Old Smoky Mountain Days

Selected Writings of

Horace Kephart
Joseph S. Hall
and
Harvey Broome

Edited and Introduced By
Arthur McDade

PANTHER PRESS
SEYMOUR, TENNESSEE

Front Cover — *"Timeless"* by renowned artist Jim Gray, whose works have depicted the beauty of the Smokies for many years. The print *"Timeless"* was produced to benefit the Smokies through Friends of Great Smoky Mountains National Park. Mr. Gray feels strongly about returning a little something to the mountains which have given him so much.

ISBN   1-887205-08-X

Introductions Copyright 1996 by Arthur McDade

Other texts are printed by permission.

PANTHER PRESS
P.O. BOX 636
SEYMOUR, TENNESSEE 37865
423-573-5792 • Fax: 423-573-5697

Dedicated to my parents who first took me to the Smokies

Arthur McDade is a park ranger/historian who is currently serving in Big South Fork National River and Recreation Area in Tennessee and Kentucky. Even though McDade has served various assignments in the National Park Service he visits the Great Smoky Mountains often. His love of the Smokies comes through in the many articles he has published in *The Tennessee Conservationist, Courier, Ranger,* and *Cultural Resources Management.*

Forward

Horace Kephart, Joseph Hall, and Harvey Broome are giants in Great Smoky Mountain literature. They all wrote to preserve what they observed and experienced. Arthur McDade has done a wonderful job in pulling together passages from books which are difficult to find. Hopefully this small volume will be an introduction to the works of these three men.

Each man worked to preserve and protect the Great Smoky Mountains. Kephart wrote and spoke for the establishment of the park. Hall listened, recorded and wrote in order to preserve the folklore and history of the Smoky's people. Broome tirelessly struggled to protect the park and other wilderness areas in the country.

The unique interests and styles of these three men can be heard in the following texts. It is truly a pleasure that these writings have been brought together to help us remember the natural and cultural history of the Great Smoky Mountains.

Listen to each man's words. Enjoy the various perspectives. Most of all revel in the wonder and beauty of Great Smoky Mountains National Park.

Charles Maynard
Executive Director
Friends of Great Smoky Mountains National Park

Table of Contents

ARTHUR McDADE   "Something Hidden; Go and Find It"

*O*ld Smoky Mountain Days. The words conjure up images of early settlers in denim bib overalls behind the reins of mule-drawn plows in tight mountain valleys. Of pioneer women spinning cotton on the front porches of dog-trot log cabins, wearing homespun dresses with bonnets. Usually in the background of our mental images flow the strains of mountain fiddle tunes, filtering through our conventional images of Appalachia as portrayed in untold Hollywood productions.

Obviously, many of our images of the southern mountain folk are stereotypical. The land and the people of the Southern Appalachians are not one-dimensional. No one perception, and certainly no one writer, can adequately describe the mountain people or the land itself. But knowledge of earlier perceptions of the mountains gives us a foundation. It can be our link to the past. In addition to admiring the uncontested beauty of the southern Appalachians, most of us are fascinated by the breed of men and women who lived in these remote valleys, called "coves" by the hill people.

The following edited works are samples of three different early perceptions of the Great Smoky Mountains and the hill people. The authors herein cover a sixty year span of observations on the people and places of these ancient hills. These writers may have disparate styles and interests, but their writings share a common bond of being early interpretations of the Smoky Mountains. These authors describe to us their love for the hills. They invite us in their unique way to "come to the mountains", as John Muir said of the Sierra Nevada range. After reading these men's work, it ought to be hard not to want to explore the Smoky Mountains.

Visit Cades Cove on a lazy summer afternoon, and sit by the Cable Mill and observe the re-creation of mountain life by the "living history" interpreters. While sitting on the porch, look off east to the main crest of the Smokies (to the "back of beyond" as Horace Kephart called it), and observe Thunderhead Mountain as a summer storm brews around its summit. Up there the settlers had their cattle in the summer, up in the cool grasses of Spence and Russell Fields.

On a hike up to those grassy "balds", you can lie in the luxurious grass of Spence Field on a hot summer day. From this prone position you get a grass-high look at the summer insects flitting through the afternoon sun, making their living in the cool environment of these high balds. It is not hard to imagine the quiet tinkling of cow bells across the meadow as the settler's cattle lethargically sauntered and ate the summer's plenty. Up there, as you idly lie and imagine, your reverie quite likely will be tempered by a distant roll of thunder from a developing summer afternoon storm. If you're lucky, your hike back down to Cades Cove will be in a surreal rainy mist, which can change the Smokies from a land of unlimited mountain vistas into a fantasy land of magical tree shapes filtering through the drifting high fog. Back in the cove, you can enter the John Oliver cabin and look out through the east-facing window at the misty slopes of Thunderhead Mountain. Maybe then, after the hike to the summit and some time in the cove, you'll get a feel for the way of life in these mountains.

A visit to the Smoky Mountains can be habit forming. I got my first view of the Great Smoky Mountains as a young boy, and all I can say, after forty years of thinking about and returning to them, is I must have fallen in love with these ancient mountains. I thank my parents for taking me to the Smokies in my youth, although my attraction to the mountains has bordered on something like an addiction over the years. Even when I was very young and could only stare up at the mountain ridges from the window of our '55 Buick, I instinctively knew that these mountains were very old and very mysterious.

The human history of these mountains is fascinating. Something about the Smoky Mountains has beckoned people for the last ten thousand years. These mountain ridges and valleys have been periodically the homes and get-away retreats of aboriginal, pioneer, and modern peoples. Like the wide-eyed kid in the 1950s looking up at the ridges from the back seat of the Buick on a family weekend, a visitor's first glimpse of the Smokies may lead to a later excursion, and then another. For whether it was a place in which to hunt and gather food in the ancient days, a place to farm in the pioneer days, or a scenic wilderness get-away for modern folk, these mountains have drawn people. They probably always will.

The edited essays compiled in this book represent three colorful and distinct interpretations of mountain life in the Great Smoky Mountains. The authors herein (Horace Kephart, Joseph S. Hall, Harvey Broome) were not casual visitors. Horace Kephart lived with the Smoky mountaineers in the early part of this century and had a particular interest in describing his neighbors. Joseph S. Hall's interest was mountain linguistics, and he travelled deep into the coves and hollows carrying his cumbersome recording device. He pioneered the study of Smoky Mountain speech. Harvey Broome, a native son of the Smokies, spent a lifetime exploring the mountains, and went on to become a national conservation leader. Their combined work provides a continuum of reflections on people and places of the mountains, from the pre-park days of Kephart, up to Harvey Broome's last essays about the high country in the late 1960s. All of their work, save Kephart's, is out of print.

The authors beckon us to come to the Smokies and relax and learn. Take this book with you to Cataloochee Valley, Oconaluftee, Deep Creek, and Cades Cove. Walk through the cemeteries in Cades Cove, Cataloochee, or along the Old Sugarland Road, and see the names of the Olivers, the McCarters, the Ogles, and the Whaleys. Visit the cabins in the coves and sit and imagine the life of these fellow Americans. Even though their's was not a sentimental and easy life in these mountain valleys, the self sufficiency and resourcefulness these people exhibited are a lasting national legacy.

Those "old Smoky Mountain days" are long gone, but not forgotten. Abandoned homesites, restored cabins, and costumed interpreters still await the visitor to the Smokies. With *imagination, and the words of the authors herein, the visitor can find something of the old Smoky days. As Horace Kephart, quoting Kipling, said of the Smokies, there is "something hidden; go and find it."*

HORACE KEPHART

"The Back of Beyond"

*T*he forces of civilization and those of wilderness sometimes try our souls. No better example of this can be found than the case of Horace Kephart. A scholarly and civilized man who channeled his intellectual energy into a successful career as a librarian in St. Louis, Missouri, Kephart enigmatically gave up his urbanized life in 1904, left his family, and moved to the Smoky Mountains to live out the last half of his life. Perhaps no other personality of these mountains is so enigmatic, and yet so fascinating.

Born in East Salem, Pennsylvania in 1862, Kephart succeeded in the world of library science, ultimately becoming the chief librarian of the St. Louis Mercantile Library. But a penchant for strong drink and an inner restlessness lurked under his veneer of success. Apparently not cut out for the domestic life of husband, father, and city dweller, Kephart took a train in 1904 to Bushnell, North Carolina (now inundated by the waters of Fontana Lake) in order to get as far back into the mountains as possible. The demons of the bottle had left him sick and despairing, and he gambled on finding a new life in the remote southern Appalachians.

He came to the Smoky Mountains precisely because of their remoteness. Of the southern Appalachians he wrote: "The most diligent research failed to discover so much as a magazine article written within this generation, that described the land and its' people. Nay, there was not even a novel or a story that showed intimate local knowledge. Had I been going to Teneriffe or Timbuctu, the libraries would have furnished information a-plenty; but about this housetop of eastern America they were strangely silent." He commenced to fill that void in the literature, and by the 1920s he was the "grand old man of the Smokies", chronicling the lives of the southern mountaineers and laying the foundation for the later establishment of the Great Smoky Mountains National Park.

Kephart knew the only way to write about the life of the mountain people was to live it. His fascination with the Cherokee Indians and the white mountaineers led him to a mountain cabin up Hazel Creek, an area which is now a part of the national park. It is important to remember that Kephart lived in the Smoky Mountains prior to the establishment of the national park; his commentary, therefore, is especially evocative of the life of the Smokies' mountaineers before the disruptions caused by the park's establishment. There is no sentimentality in the rendering of his subjects.

His writing produced two classics. In Camping and Woodcraft *he evokes the feeling of adventure and exploration of the "mountain men" of the West, and the survival skills of the Indians.* Our Southern Highlanders *describes the colorful Southern Appalachian mountain dwellers, and put Kephart on the literary map with its publication in 1913. He became sought after by visitors and autograph seekers, and would escape from the solicitations of these people by retreating to his mountain cabin or turning to the bottle.*

By today's standards, Kephart's writing may sound somewhat archaic. He often uses references to persons, historic events, and writers which are not well known to today's reader. His prose can be flowery and rhythmical, full of exclamation points, extensive adjectives and parenthetical expressions. We have to remember the tenor of the times in which he wrote. Even the great naturalist John Muir's writings reflect a style that is out of vogue today.

Kephart's life appears to have had a "Dr. Jekyll and Mr. Hyde" quality. On the one hand his writings reveal an engaged and articulate observer of his adopted mountains. But he was tormented at times with his interior demons and would sink into black depressions, in which alcohol sometimes became his solace. Ironically, this would lead to his death. In

1931 Kephart was killed in an auto accident near Bryson City, North Carolina while reportedly returning from a bootlegger. He was buried in a hilltop cemetery overlooking Spring and Main Streets in Bryson City. Below his grave site in the town today there is a state historical marker dedicated to him, in addition to a stream and a mountain named after him in the Great Smoky Mountains National Park.

It is important to note that Kephart makes some sweeping generalizations about the mountain folk in Our Southern Highlanders *that are based more on personal opinion than fact. Some recent research suggests that the mountain people were not as isolated as Kephart suggests. The book is his own interpretation based on his contacts with the hill people; it is not necessarily the definitive interpretation. This notwithstanding, his book is an early and colorful evocation of the mountains, and an important foundation of the bibliography on the Smoky Mountains.*

In the following passages from Our Southern Highlanders *Kephart paints a picture of the mountaineer's life. Read it and then visit Deep Creek, Hazel Creek, and Cataloochee on the North Carolina side of the national park, and Cades Cove on the Tennessee side. Walk up the quiet drainages and see the abandoned cabin sites with their skeletal chimneys remaining* as stark reminders of the homes of real people. I think you'll agree that Kephart's colorful prose and characterizations of the hill people make interesting reading.

HORACE KEPHART

"The Great Smoky Mountains"
(From *Our Southern Highlanders*)

For a long time my chief interest was not in human neighbors but in the mountains themselves -in that mysterious beckoning hinterland which rose right back of my chimney and spread upward, outward, almost to three cardinal points of the compass, mile after mile, hour after hour of lusty climbing — an Eden still unpeopled and unspoiled.

I loved of a morning to slip on my haversack, pick up my rifle, or maybe a mere staff, and stride forth alone over haphazard routes, to enjoy in my own untutored way the infinite variety of form and color and shade, of plant and tree and animal life, in that superb wilderness that towered there far above all homes of men. (And I love it still, albeit the charm of new discovery is gone from those heights and gulfs that are now so intimate and full of memories).

The Carolina mountains have a character all their own. Rising abruptly from a low base, and then rounding more gradually upward for 2,000-5,000 feet above their valleys, their apparent height is more impressive than that of many a loftier summit in the West which forms only a protuberance on an elevated plateau. Nearly all of them are clad to their tops in dense forest and thick undergrowth. Here and there is a grassy "bald": a natural meadow curiously perched on the very top of a mountain. There are no bare, rocky summits rising above timberline, few jutting crags, no ribs and vertebrae of the earth exposed. Seldom does one see even a naked ledge of rock. The very cliffs are sheathed with trees and shrubs, so that one treading their edges has no fear of falling into an abyss.

Pinnacles or serrated ridges are rare. There are few commanding peaks. From almost any summit in Carolina one looks out upon a sea of flowing curves and dome-shaped eminences undulating, with no great disparity of height, unto the horizon. Almost everywhere the contours are similar: steep sides gradually rounding to the tops, smooth-surfaced to the eye because of the endless verdure. Every ridge is separated from its sisters by deep and narrow ravines. Not one of the thousand water courses shows a glint of its dashing stream, save where some far-off river may reveal, through a gap in the mountain, one single shimmering curve. In all this vast

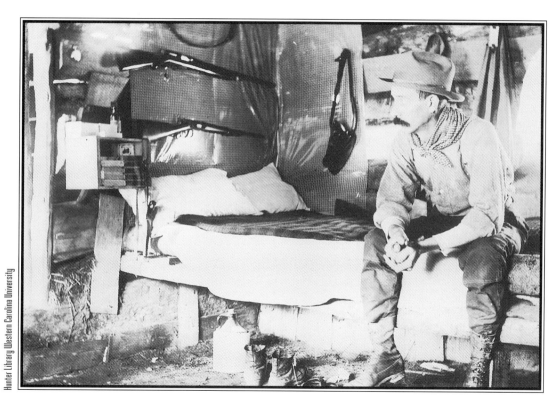

Kephart on Bunk in Hall Cabin — Siler's Meadow

prospect, a keen eye, knowing where to look, may detect an occasional farmer's clearing, but to the stranger there is only mountain and forest, mountain and forest, as far as the eye can reach.

Characteristic, too, is the dreamy blue haze, like that of Indian summer intensified, that ever hovers over the mountains, unless they be swathed in cloud, or, for a few minutes, after a sharp rain-storm has cleared the atmosphere. Both the Blue Ridge and the Smoky Mountains owe their names to this tenuous mist. It softens all outlines, and lends a mirage-like effect of great distance to objects that are but a few miles off, while those farther removed grow more and more intangible until finally the sky-line blends with the sky itself.

The foreground of such a landscape, in summer, is warm, soft, dreamy, caressing, habitable; beyond it are gentle and luring solitudes; the remote ranges are inexpressibly lonesome, isolated and mysterious; but everywhere the green forest mantle bespeaks a vital present; nowhere does cold, bare granite stand as the sepulchre of an immemorial past.

And yet these very mountains of Carolina are among the ancients of the earth.

They were old, very old, before the Alps and the Andes, the Rockies and the Himalayas were molded into their primal shapes. Upon them, in after ages, were born the first hardwoods of America — perhaps those of Europe, too — and upon them today the last great hardwood forests of our country stand in primeval majesty, mutely awaiting their imminent doom.

The richness of the Great Smoky forests has been the wonder and the admiration of everyone who has traversed it. As one climbs from the river to one of the main peaks, he passes successively through the same floral zones he would encounter in traveling from mid-Georgia to southern Canada.

Starting amid sycamores, elms, gums, willows, persimmons, chinquapins, he soon enters a region of beech, birch, basswood, magnolia, cucumber, butternut, holly, sourwood, box elder, ash, maple, buckeye, poplar, hemlock, and a great number of other growths along the creeks and branches. On the lower slopes are many species of oaks, with hickory, hemlock, pitch pine, locust, dogwood, and chestnut. In this region nearly all trees attain their fullest development. On north fronts of hills the oaks reach a diameter of five to six feet. In cool, rich coves, chestnut trees grow from six to nine feet across the stump; and tulip poplars up to ten to eleven feet, their straight trunks towering like gigantic columns, with scarcely a noticeable taper, seventy or eighty feet to the nearest limb.

Ascending above the zone of 3,000 feet, white oak is replaced by the no less valuable "mountain oak." Beech, birch, buckeye, and chestnut persist to 5,000 feet. Then, where the beeches dwindle until adult trees are only knee-high, there begins a sub-arctic zone of black spruce, balsam, striped maple, aspen, and the "Peruvian" or red cherry.

I have named only a few of the prevailing growths. Nowhere else in the temperate zone is there such a variety of merchantable timber as in western Carolina and the Tennessee front of the Unaka system. About a hundred and twenty species of native trees grow in the Smoky forest itself. When Asa Gray visited the North Carolina mountains he identified, in a thirty mile trip, a greater variety of indigenous trees than could be observed in crossing Europe from England to Turkey, or in a trip from Boston to the Rocky Mountain plateau. As John Muir has said, our forests, "however slighted by man, must have been a great delight to God; for they were the best He ever planted."

The undergrowth is of almost tropical luxuriance and variety. Botanists say that this is the richest collecting ground in the United States. Whether one be seeking ferns or fungi or orchards or almost anything else vegetal, each hour will bring him some new delight. In summer the upper mountains are one vast flower garden: the white and pink of rhododendron, the blaze of azalea, conspicuous above all else, in settings of every imaginable shade of green.

It was the botanist who discovered this Eden for us. Far back in the eighteenth century, when this was still "Cherokee Country", inhabited by no whites but a few Indian-traders, William Bartram of Philadelphia came plant-hunting into the mountains of western Carolina, and spread their fame to the world. One of his choicest finds was the fiery azalea, of which he recorded: "The epithet 'fiery' I annex to this most celebrated species of azalea, as being expressive of the appearance of its flowers; which are in general of the color of the finest red-lead, orange, and bright gold, as well as yellow and cream-color. These various splendid colors are not only in separate plants, but frequently all the varieties and shades are seen in separate branches on the same plant; and the clusters of the blossoms cover the shrubs in such incredible profusion on the hillsides that, suddenly opening to view from dark shades, we are alarmed with apprehension of the woods being set on fire."

The most rugged and difficult part of the Smokies (and of the United States east of Colorado) is in the sawtooth mountains between Collins and Guyot (Editor's note: Mt. Collins and Mt. Guyot), at the headwaters of the Okona Lufty (Oconaluftee) River. I know but few men who have ever followed this part of the divide, although during the present year trails have been put from Clingman (Clingman's Dome) to Collins, or near it, and possibly others beyond to the northeastward.

In August and September, 1900, Mr. James H. Ferris and wife, naturalists from Joliet, Illinois, explored the Smokies to the Lufty Gap northeast of Clingman, collecting rare species of snails and ferns. No doubt Mrs. Ferris is the only white woman who ever went beyond Clingman or even ascended the Dome itself. She stayed at the Lufty Gap while her husband and a Carolina mountaineer of my acquaintance struggled through to Guyot and returned. Of this trip Mr. Ferris sent me the following account:

"We bought another axe off a moonshiner, and, with a week's provisions on our backs, one of the guides and I took the 'Consolidated American Black Bear and Ruffed Grouse Line' for Mount Guyot, twenty miles farther by map measurement. The bears were in full possession of the property, and we could get no information in the settlements, as the settlers do not travel this line. They did not know the names of the peaks other than as tops of the Great Smokies-knew nothing of the character of the country except that it was rough. The Tennesseeans seem afraid of the mountains, and the Cherokees of the North Carolina side equally so; for, two miles from camp, all traces of man, except surveyor's marks, had disappeared. In the first two days we routed eight bears out of their nests and mud wallows, and they seemed to stay routed, for upon our return we found the blackberry crop unharvested and had a bag pudding- "duff" — or what you call it.

"A Surveyor had run part of the line this year, which helped us greatly, and the bears had made well-beaten trails part of the way. In places they had mussed up the ground as much as a barnyard. We tried to follow the boundary line between the two States, which is exactly upon the tip of the Smokies, but often missed it. The government [state] surveyor many years ago made two hacks upon the trees, but sometimes the linemen neglected to use their axes for half a mile or so. It took us three and one-half days to go, and two and one-half to return, and we arose with the morning star and worked hard all day. The last day and a half, going, there was nothing to guide us but the old hacks.

"Equipped with government maps, a good compass, and a little conceit, I thought I could follow the boundary line. In fact, at one time we intended to go through without a guide. A trail that runs through blackberry bushes two miles out of three is hard to follow. Then there was a huckleberry bush reaching to our waists growing thickly upon the ground as tomato vines, curled hard, and stubborn; and laurel much like a field of lilac bushes, crooked and strong as iron. In one place we walked fully a quarter of a mile over the tops of laurel bushes and these were ten or twelve feet in height, but blown over one way by the wind. Much of the trail was along rocky edges, sometimes but six inches or so wide, but almost straight down on both sides for hundreds of feet. One night, delayed by lack of water, we did not camp till dark, and, finding a smooth spot, lay down with a small log on each side to hold us from rolling out of bed. When daylight came we found that, had we rolled over the logs, my partner would have dropped 500 feet into Tennessee and I would have dropped as far into North Carolina, unless some friendly tree top had caught us. Sometimes the mountain forked, and these ridges, concealed by the balsams, would not be seen. Then there were round knobs — and who can tell where the highest ridge lies on a round mountain or a ball? My woolen shirt was torn off to the shoulders, and my partner, who had started out with corduroys, stayed in the brush until I got him a pair of overalls from camp."

Even to the west of Clingman a stranger is likely to find some desperately rough travel if he should stray from the trail that follows the divide. It is easy going for anyone in fair weather, but when clouds settle on the mountain, as it often does without warning, it may be so thick that one cannot see a tree ten feet away. Under such circumstances I have myself floundered from daylight till dark through heart-breaking laurel thickets, and without a bite to eat, not knowing whither I was going except that it was toward the Little Tennessee River.

In 1906 I spent the summer in a herder's hut on top of the divide, just west of the

Locust Ridge (miscalled Chestnut Ridge on the map), about six miles east of Thunderhead. This time I had a partner, and we had a glorious three months of it, nearly a mile above sea level, and only half a day's climb from the nearest settlement. One day I was alone, Andy having gone down to Medlin for the mail. It had rained a good deal — in fact, there was a shower nearly every day throughout the summer, the only semblance of a dry season in the Smokies being the autumn and early winter. The nights were cold enough for fires and blankets, even in our well chinked cabin.

Well, I had finished my lonesome dinner, and was washing up, when I saw a man approaching. This was an event, for we seldom saw other men than our two selves. He was a lame man, wearing an iron extension on one foot, and he bobbled with a cane. He looked played-out and gaunt. I met him outside. He smiled as though I looked good to him, and asked with some eagerness, "Can I buy something to eat here?"

"No," I answered, "you can't buy anything here" — how his face fell! — "but I'll give you the best we have, and you're welcome."

Then you should have seen that smile!

He seemed to have just enough strength left to drag himself into the hut. I asked no questions, though wondering what a cripple, evidently a gentleman, though in rather bad repair, was doing on top of the Smoky Mountains. It was plain that he had spent more than one night shelterless in the cold rain, and that he was quite famished. While I was baking the biscuit and cooking some meat, he told his story. This is the short of it:

"I am a Canadian, McGill University man, electrician. My company sent me to Cincinnati. I got a vacation of a couple of weeks, and thought I'd take a pedestrian tour. I can walk better than you'd think," and he tapped the short leg.

I liked his grit.

"I knew no place to go," he continued; "so I took a map and looked for what might be interesting country, not too far from Cincinnati. I picked out these mountains, got a couple of government topographical sheets, and, thinking they would serve like European ordnance maps, I had no fear of going astray. It was my plan to walk through to the Balsam Mountains, and so on to the Big Pigeon River. I went to

Maryville, Tennessee, and there I was told that I would find a cabin every five or six miles along the summit from Thunderhead to the Balsams."

I broke in abruptly: "Whoever told you that was either an imposter or an ignoramus. There are only four of these shacks on the whole Smoky range. Two of them, the Russell cabin and the Spence place, you have already passed without knowing it. This is called the Hall cabin. None of these three are occupied save for a week or so in the fall when the cattle are being rounded up, or by chance, as my partner and I happen to be here now. Beyond this there is just one shack, at Siler's Meadow. It is down below the summit, hidden in timber, and you would have found it as bare as a last year's mouse nest, for nobody ever goes there except a few bear hunters. From there onward for forty miles is an uninhabited wilderness so tough that you could not make seven miles a day in it save your life, even if you knew the course; and there is no trail at all. Those government maps are good and reliable to show the approaches to this wild country, but where you need them most they are good for nothing."

"Then," said he, "if I had missed your cabin I would have starved to death, for I depended on finding a house to the eastward, and would have followed the trail till

I dropped. I have been out in the laurel thickets, now, three days and two nights; so nothing could have induced me to leave this trail, once I found it, or until I could see out to a house on one side or other of the mountain."

"You would see no house on either side from here to beyond Guyot (ed. note: Mt. Guyot), about forty miles. Had you no rations at all?"

"I traveled light, expecting to find entertainment among the native. Here is what I have left." He showed me a crumpled buckwheat flapjack, a pinch of tea, and a couple of ounces of brandy.

"I was saving them for the last extremity; have had nothing to eat since yesterday morning. Drink the brandy, please; it came from Montreal."

"No, my boy, that liquor goes down your own throat instanter. You're the chap that needs it. This coffee will boil now in a minute. I won't give you all the food you want, for it wouldn't be prudent; but by and by you shall have a bellyfull."

Then, as well as he could, he sketched the route he had followed. Where the trail from Tennessee crosses from Thunderhead to Haw Gap he had swerved off from the divide, and he discovered his error somewhere in the neighborhood of Blockhouse.

There, instead of retracing his steps, he sought a short cut by plunging down to the headwaters of Haw Creek, thus worming deeper and deeper to the devil's nest. One more day would have finished him. When I told him that the trip from Clingman to Guyot would be hard work for a party of experienced mountaineers, and that it would probably take them a week, during which time they would have to pack all supplies on their own backs, he agreed that his best course would be down into Carolina and out to the railroad.

HORACE KEPHART

Who Are the Mountaineers?
(From *Our Southern Highlanders*)

*T*he Southern Appalachian Mountains happen to be parceled out among eight different states, and for that reason they are seldom considered as a geographical unit. In the same way their inhabitants are thought of as Kentucky mountaineers or Carolina mountaineers, but not often as a body of Appalachian mountaineers. And yet these inhabitants are as distinct an ethnographic group as the mountains themselves are a geographic group.

The mountaineers are homogeneous so far as speech and manners and experiences and ideals can make them. In the aggregate they are nearly twice as numerous and cover twice as much territory as any one of the States among which they have been distributed; but in each of these States they occupy only the backyard, and generally take back seats in the councils of the commonwealth. They have been fenced off from each other by political boundaries, and have no such coherence among themselves as would come from common leadership or a sense of common origin and mutual dependence.

And they are a people without annals. "Borned in the kentry and ain't never been out o' hit" is all that most of them can say for themselves. Here and there one will assert, "My foreparents war principally Scotch," or "Us Bumgyarners [Baumgartners] was Dutch," but such traditions of a far-back foreign origin are uncommon.

Who are these southern mountaineers? Whence came they? What is the secret of their belatedness and isolation?

Before the Civil War they were seldom heard of in the outside world. Vaguely it was understood that the Appalachian highlands were occupied by a peculiar people called "mountain whites." This odd name was given them not to distinguish them from mountain negroes, for there were, practically, no mountain negroes; but to indicate their similarity, in social condition and economic status, to the "poor whites" of the southern lowlands. It was assumed, on no historical basis whatever, that the highlanders came from the more venturesome or desperate element of the "poor whites", and differed from these only to the extent that environment had shaped them.

Since this theory still prevails throughout the South, and is accepted generally elsewhere on its face value, it deserves just enough consideration to refute it.

View of Cabin at Siler's Meadow (Siler's Bald)

The unfortunate class known as poor whites in the South is descended mainly from the convicts and indentured servants with which England supplied labor to the southern plantations before slavery days. The Cavaliers who founded and dominated southern society came from the conservative, feudal element of England. Their character and training were essentially aristocratic and military. They were not town-dwellers, but masters of plantations. Their chief crop and article of export was tobacco. The culture of tobacco required an abundance of cheap and servile labor.

Thus a considerable proportion of the white laborers of the South, in the seventeenth century, were criminals or ne'er-do-wells from the start. A large number of the others came from the dregs of society. As for the remainder, the companionships into which they were thrust, the brutalities to which they were subjected, their impotence before the law, the contempt in which they were held by the ruling caste, were enough to undermine all but the strongest characters. Few ever succeeded in rising to respectable position.

These white freedmen generally became squatters on such land as was unfit for tobacco, cotton, and other crops profitable to slave-owners. As the plantations expanded, these freedmen were pushed further and further back upon more and more sterile soil. They became "pine-landers", or "piney-woods people", "sand-hillers", or "crackers".

Now these poor whites had nothing to do with settling the mountains. There was then, and still is, plenty of wild land for them in their native lowlands. The mountains, to those who had ever heard of them, suggested nothing but laborious climbing amid mysterious and portentous perils. They never entered Appalachia until after it had been won and settled by a far manlier race, and even then they went only in driblets. The theory that the southern mountains were peopled mainly by outcasts from the old settlements in the lowlands rests on no other basis than imagination.

The first frontiersmen of the Appalachians were those Swiss and Germans who began flocking into Transylvania about 1682. They settled westward of the Quakers in the fertile limestone belts at the foot of the Blue Ridge and the Alleghanies.

Shortly after the tide of German immigration set into Pennsylvania, another and quite different class of foreigners began to arrive in this province, attracted by the same lodestones that drew the Germans, namely, democratic institutions and religious liberty. These newcomers were the Scotch-Irish, or Ulstermen of Ireland.

So it was that these people became, in their turn, our westernmost frontiersmen, taking up land just outside the German settlements. Immediately they began to clash with the Indians, and there followed a long series of border wars, waged with extreme ferocity, in which sometimes it is hard to say which side was most to blame. One thing, however, is certain: if any race was ordained to exterminate the Indians that race was the Scotch-Irish.

HORACE KEPHART

The People of the Hills
(From *Our Southern Highlanders*)

*I*n delineating a strange race we are prone to disregard what is common in our own experience and observe sharply what is odd. The oddities we sketch and remember and tell about. But there is little danger of misrepresenting the physical features and mental traits of the hill people, because among them there is one definite type that greatly predominates. This is not to be wondered at when we remember that fully three-fourths of our highlanders are practically of the same descent, have lived the same kind of life for generations, and have intermarried to a degree unknown in other parts of America.

Our average mountaineer is lean, inquisitive, shrewd. If that be what constitutes a Yankee, as is popularly supposed outside of New England, then this Yankee of the South is as true to the type as the conventional Uncle Sam himself.

A fat mountaineer is a curiosity. Spartan diet does not put on flesh. Still, it should be noted that long legs, baggy clothing, and scantiness of underwear make people seem thinner than they really are. Our highlanders are conspicuously a tall race. About two-thirds of them are brawny or sinewy fellows of great endurance. The others generally are slab-sided, stoop-shouldered, but withey. The townsfolk and the valley farmers, being better nourished and more observant of the prime laws of wholesome living, are noticeably superior in appearance but not in stamina.

Nearly all males of the back country have a grave and deliberate bearing. They travel with the long, sure-footed stride of the born woodsman, not graceful and lithe like a moccasined Indian (their course brogans forbid it), but shambling as if every joint had too much play. There is nothing about them to suggest the Swiss or Tyrolean mountaineers; rather they resemble the gillies of the Scotch Highlands. Generally they are lean-faced, sallow, level-browed, with rather high cheek bones. Gray eyes predominate, sometimes vacuous, but oftener hard, searching, crafty-the feral eye of primitive man.

Many of the women are pretty in youth; but hard toil in house and field, early marriage, frequent child-bearing with shockingly poor attention, and ignorance or defiance of the plainest necessities of hygiene, soon warp and age them. At thirty or thirty-five a mountain woman is apt to have a worn and faded look, with form prematurely bent — and what wonder? Always bending over the hoe in the cornfields, or bending over the hearth as she cooks by an open fire, or bending over her baby, or bending to pick up, for the thousandth time, the wet duds that her lord flings on the floor as he enters from the woods — what wonder that she soon grows short-waisted and round-shouldered?

The voices of the highland women, low toned by habit, often are singularly sweet, being pitched in a sad, musical, minor key. With strangers, the women are wont to be shy, but speculative rather than timid, as they glance betimes with "a slow, long look of mild inquiry, or of general listlessness, or of unconscious and unaccountable melancholy." Many, however, scrutinize a visitor calmly for minutes at a time or frankly measure him with the gypsy eye of Carmen.

As a class, they have great and restless physical energy. Considering the quantity and quality of what they eat there is no people who can beat them in endurance of strain and privation. They are great walkers and carriers of burdens. Before there was a tub-mill in our settlement one of my neighbors used to go, every other week, thirteen miles to mill, carrying a two-bushel sack of corn (112 pounds) and returning with his meal on the following day. This was done without any pack strap but simply shifting the load from one shoulder to the other.

One of our women, known as "Long Goody" (I measured her; six feet three inches she stood) walked eighteen miles across the Smokies into Tennessee, crossing at an elevation of 5,000 feet, merely to shop more advantageously than she could at home. The next day she shouldered fifty pounds of flour and some other groceries, and bore them home before nightfall. Uncle Jimmy Crawford, in his seventy-second year, came to join a party of us on a bear hunt. He walked twelve miles across the mountain, carrying his equipment and four days rations for himself and dogs. Finding that we had gone on ahead of him he followed to our camp on Siler's Bald, twelve more miles, climbing another 3,000 feet, much of it by bad trail, finished the twenty-four mile trip in seven hours — and then wanted to turn in and help cut the nightwood. Young mountaineers afoot easily outstrip a horse on a day's journey by road and trail.

In a climate where it showers about two days out of three through spring and summer the women go about, like the men, unshielded from the wet. If you expostulate, one will laugh and reply: "I ain't sugar, nor salt, nor nobody's honey." Slickers are worn only on horseback — and two-thirds of our people had no horses. A man who was so eccentric as to carry an umbrella is known to this day as "Umbrell" John Walker.

In winter, one sometimes may see adults and children go barefoot in snow that is ankle deep. It used to be customary in our settlement to do the morning chores barefooted in the snow. "Then," said one, "our feet'd tingle and burn, so't they wouldn't git a bit cold all day when we put our shoes on." I knew a family whose children had no shoes all one winter, and occasionally we had zero weather.

There is a wealthy man known to everyone around Waynesville {ed. note: Waynesville, North Carolina}, who, being asked where he resided, as a witness in court, answered: "Three, four miles up and down Jonathan Creek." The judge was about to fine him for contempt, when it developed that the witness spoke literal truth. He lives neither in house nor camp, but perambulates his large estate and when night comes lies down wherever he may happen to be. In winter he has been known to go where some of his pigs bedded in the woods, usurp the middle for himself, and borrow comfort from their bodily heat.

HORACE KEPHART

Mountain Medicine
(From *Our Southern Highlanders*)

W hen I lived up in the Smokies there was no doctor within sixteen miles (and then, none who ever had attended a medical school). It was inevitable that my first-aid kit and limited knowledge of medicine should be requisitioned until I became a sort of "doctor to the settlement." My services, being free, at once became popular, and there was no escape; for, if I treated the Smiths, let us say, and ignored a call from the Robinsons, the slight would be resented by all Robinson connections throughout the land. So my normal occupations often were interrupted by such calls as these:

"John's Lize Ann she ain't much; cain't you-uns give her some easin'-powder for that hurtin' in her chist?"

"Right sensibly atween the shoulders I've got a pain; somethin's gone wrong with my stummick; I don't 'pear to have no stren'th left; and sometimes I'm nigh siffli-cated. Whut you reckon ails me?"

"Come right over to Mis' Fullwiler's, quick; she's fell down and busted a rib inside o' her!"

It was here that I first heard of "tooth-jumping." Let one of my old neighbors tell it in his own way:

"You take a cut nail (not one o' those round wire nails) and place it squar p'int agin the ridge of the tooth, jest under the edge of the gum. Then jump the tooth out with a hammer. A man who knows how can jump a tooth without it hurtin' half as bad as pullin'. But old Uncle Neddy Cyarter went to jump one of his own teeth out, one time, and missed the nail and mashed his nose with the hammer. He had the weak trembles."

"I have heard of tooth-jumping," said I, "and reported it to dentists back home, but they laughed at me."

"Well, they needn't laugh; for it's so. Some men git to be as experienced at it as tooth-dentists are at pullin'. They cut around the gum, and then put the nail at jest sich an angle."

"Will the tooth come at the first lick?"

"Generally. If it didn't, you might as well stick your head in a swarm of bees and ferget who you are."

HORACE KEPHART

Mountain Religion
(From *Our Southern Highlanders*)

*T*he mountaineers are intensely, universally Protestant. You will seldom find a backwoodsman who knows what a Roman Catholic is. As John Fox {ed. note: Fox was a writer on mountain folkways} says, "He is the only man in the world whom the Catholic Church has made little or no effort to proselyte. Dislike of Episcopalianism is still strong among people who do not know, or pretend not to know, what the word means. 'Any Episcopalians around here?', asked a clergyman at a mountain cabin. "I don't know," said the old woman. "Jim's got the skins of a lot o' varmints up in the loft. Mebbe you can find one up thar."

Nearly all of our highlanders, from youth upward, show an amazing fondness for theological dispute. This consists mainly in capping texts, instead of reasoning, with the single-minded purpose of confusing or downing an opponent. Into this battle of memories rather than wits the most worthless scapegrace will enter with keen gusto and perfect seriousness. I have known two or three hundred mountain lumberjacks, hard swearing and hard drinking "tough-as-they-make-'ems", to be whetted to a fighting edge over the rocky problem "Was Saul damned? (Can a suicide enter the kingdom of heaven?)

I have seen the worst as well as the best of Appalachia.

There are "places on Sand Mountain" — scores of them — where unspeakable orgies prevail at times. But I know that the great mass of the mountain people are very like persons of similar station elsewhere, just human, with human frailties, only a little more honest, I think, in owning them. And even in the tenebra of far-back coves, where conditions exist as gross as anything to be found in the wynds and closes of our great cities, there is this blessed difference: that these half-wild creatures have not been driven into desperate war against society. The worst of them still have good traits, strong characters, something responsive to decent treatment. They are kind-hearted, loyal to their friends, quick to help anyone in distress. They know nothing of civilization. They are simply the unstarted.

Joseph S. Hall   "Let the Mountain People Tell Their Own Stories"

I n 1960 an obscure writer produced a small booklet on the mountain folk of the Great Smokies. In a mere 69 pages the author, a former seasonal government folklorist, related his experiences in the Smokies in the summer of 1937, during the great public works period which spawned the Civilian Conservation Corps (CCC) and the Works Progress Administration (WPA). The book, titled Smoky Mountain Folks And Their Lore, *had an initial limited printing not uncommon for regional folklore studies, and was available in the Great Smoky Mountains Natural History Association bookstores as late as 1977. Never intended as an exhaustive study, the book nevertheless filled a folklore gap in the interpretation of the hill people of the Great Smokies. With its inexpensive price and short length, it reached a large audience of park visitors. With the book's publication, Joseph S. Hall continued the tradition of Horace Kephart as a chronicler of the Smoky Mountain hill people and their ways.*

Joseph Sargent Hall was born in Butte, Montana on August 22, 1906. His father, a physician, moved the family to southern California in 1908, where Joseph S. Hall grew up.

He studied English in college, and grew especially intrigued with linguistics, which ultimately led to his association with the mountain people of the Smokies. As a fresh graduate school product of Columbia University, he accepted a government job in June 1937 which led him by train through Virginia into the Tennessee Valley to Gatlinburg (in those days, the town was anything but the bustling tourist town of today). Off and on from 1937 to 1956 Joseph S. Hall toured the Great Smoky Mountains National Park in search of folklore. What started as a minor government job documenting the life of the settlers in the Smokies during the CCC and WPA years led to a twenty year interest in the folklore of the Smoky Mountains.

Hall's first summer in the Smokies started at the CCC camp near park headquarters, where he bunked with the workers at night, by day hitched rides deep into the Smokies on the CCC's big stake™ bodied trucks. Coming upon some farm house or other dwelling, Hall would disembark the truck and walk up and attempt to interview the homesteaders. Hall talked to people who "lived so fur back in the hills they use possums to carry the mail and lightnin' bugs for lanterns." Over the summer, Hall interviewed tens of families who generally opened up their homes and lives to the "furriner". As he progressed in his work, Hall

began to realize that he was engaged in "one of the most rewarding periods of my life, a period of adventure and of great human interest, and of contribution, I hope, to the cause of preserving the oral lore of this region."

Hall's special interest was linguistics. His work was dedicated to collecting "information on mountain dialect in the Smokies through conversation with the people, by hearing them describe old ways of life, recount memorable events of the past, and tell folk tales and tall tales, utter proverbial sayings, and the like." The project was not merely an intellectual exercise; an urgency was added by the fact that most of the mountain residents soon would be moved from the national park to new homes in neighboring valleys.

In addition to Smoky Mountain Folks And Their Lore, Hall wrote Sayings From Old Smoky, Yarns And Tales From The Great Smokies, an several unpublished manuscripts on mountain folklore.

Hall let the mountain folk speak for themselves. He made no attempt to authenticate or change any facts related to any event. As he said in his introduction to Smoky Mountain Folks And Their Lore, "it has been the desire all along to let the mountain people tell their own stories."

Hall died on February 14, 1992 in Oceanside, California. His legacy can be summed up in the words of Professor Michael Montgomery of the University of South Carolina: "Joseph Hall was the pioneer researcher of the speech and culture of the Great Smoky Mountains of Tennessee and North Carolina."

So sit back now and let the mountain folk tell their own stories.

Joseph S. Hall

"That's the Way Old-Timey Folks Talked"
(From *Smoky Mountain Folks And Their Lore*)
Smokies Dialect
Disappearance of the Old Smokies Life

*I*f there is any one thing which illustrates simply and well a people's character or group personality, it is the language they use. If their speech is a dialect of a standard language, the linguistic reflection of their personality appears in even stronger outlines than otherwise. There are colorful local or regional words, words elsewhere outmoded, but often full of pictures of folk imagery.

I would like to reveal something of the life of the Smokies people by telling some of their linguistic traditions. The Smokies people and their language are practically matters of history now, for most of the area became a national park in 1934 and almost none of the original population reside within the park boundaries now. The very few exceptions are some of the Park personnel and their families who were born and raised there, and a few families in the scenic Cades Cove who have been allowed to stay to sow the broad fields in hay and to keep their cattle in order to preserve

Joseph S. Hall as a graduate student

some of the trim, agricultural neatness characteristic of this valley before the park era. Back in 1937, when a number of elderly people had been given leases allowing them to spend the rest of their days on their old home places, Mrs. Docia Styles of Indian Creek told me about her lease. She said, "They told me I could stay as long as I lived. I told 'em that would be as long as I wanted to stay."

My studies were carried on mainly in 1937-1940, while there were still several hundred native residents in the park. I interviewed as many of them as possible. Also I talked to and gathered information from great numbers of people who lived just beyond the boundaries of the park, as in Gatlinburg, Emerts Cove, and on Cosby Creek. Many of these people are still living and have assisted me with my more recent collecting. Some of these people had moved down to the bordering valleys and coves when their farms and homes were bought by the Park Commission. Nevertheless, despite the people living in the fringe areas, it must be said that the old Smokies people and their life are things of the past. The few old-timers still alive have merged their ways of living in the customs of the less mountainous, more accessible countryside and towns roundabout. Besides, for people everywhere — in towns and cities, in the Southern Appalachians generally, on the prairies of Missouri and Nebraska, on isolated farms and ranches of the Far West — times have changed. A series of general social changes has been brought about for everybody by such things as the automobile, the movies, radio, television, etc.

Into the Smokies region, besides the Park itself, have come the gigantic Tennessee Valley Authority and the huge atomic energy plant at Oak Ridge. The TVA filled wide, fertile valleys with lakes for producing power, displaced large rural settlements (with accompanying social and human pains), provided thousands of new jobs and opportunities, and in general revolutionized life in areas of the South far distant from East Tennessee. Added to these disruptive forces was the Manhattan Engineering District at Oak Ridge, which during World War II created a community of 75,000 people, intermingling residents of the Tennessee Valley with people from all over the country.

Some of these changes have been humanly illustrated by North Callahan in his American Folkways book *Smoky Mountain Country* (N.Y., 1952). This author tells (p. 176) of a bootlegger who, living in contentment in the Smokies, operated his still beside a creek when all the land round about was bought for the new national park:

"The 'legger' had to move. He went to Union County, where he resumed his occupation of making moonshine. After being there a few years, the TVA moved in and took his land for the Norris Dam basin. He next moved down on the Clinch River, and there was again engaged in his favorite vocation when the Oak Ridge project came along. This was the last straw.

"Used to be, the only federal men I dealt with was the revenoors," he snorted, "and we understood each other. Now it seems that every time I come home from a run, they's a guvermint man a-settin on my doorstep with papers orderin' me to move. If I knowed of a place where there weren't no guvermint men but revenoors, I'd shore go there."

Of the changes wrought by TVA Callahan says (pp. 177-178):

"First of all, it brought electric power where it had never been available before. Probably next in importance was the cheap fertilizer it provided farmers."

In sum, we have a picture of two to three million tourists soaking up the beauties of the area every year, industrialization springing up throughout the whole region, "furriners" from all over working and settling there, and improved standards of living. There are also increased education and (through the county bookmobiles) increased reading of books, and general modernization of living. As a consequence, there has been rapid elimination of the colorful aspects of old Smokies life, including the hearty, rugged, and picturesque dialect.

But as interesting as is the subject of social living in transition, it is not the present subject of discussion. My purpose in giving some of these details was to show how life in the Tennessee and North Carolina Appalachians is becoming radically changed, and to contrast with the flux of modern conditions the much more static, frontierlike conditions which prevailed in life and language before civilization and industry came to the mountains.

*I*t is impossible to characterize the old Smokies speech by giving a few isolated words; abundant examples of syntax, rhythmic and intonation patterns, and idioms, as well as an extensive vocabulary, are required to illustrate the nature of this mountain dialect. However, the vocabulary — the words which people employ in everyday life — does show something about the life of the speakers, their interests, concerns, and imagination.

Some of the interesting terms apply to **topography:**

Bald: a treeless mountain top characteristic of the Smokies, as in Bearwallow Bald.

Balsam: a mountaintop in the Balsam mountains, as in Cataloochee Balsam.

Bench: a level area, sometimes cultivated, on the side of a mountain.

Branch: a small stream, as in Woolly Tops Branch.

Butt: the abrupt end of a mountain ridge, as in Mollies Butt, at the end of Mollies Ridge.

Cat Heads: biscuits.

Cold Trailer: a dog which can pick up or follow a cold trail.

Corn Pones: a flat loaf of corn bread.

Cove: a widening out of a mountain valley, or a meadowland between mountains, as in Cades Cove, and Emerts Cove.

Chimley: chimney.

Croup: a cough.

Drain *(nearly always pronounced **dreen**)*: a small spring with little water, on a mountainside or in a little hollow.

Fork and Prong: important tributaries of a creek or river as in Ravens Fork, or Kephart Prong.

Fitified: as in Fitified Springs, an intermittent spring.

Gap: a depression on a ridge, as in Newfound Gap.

Hollow *(pronounced **holler**)*: a small valley, as in Pretty Hollow.

Knob: a mountain top, as in Brier Knob, Lufty Knob.

Lead: a long ridge, usually extending from a higher ridge, as in Twenty Mile Lead.

Middlin' Of Bacon: "side meat" or side of bacon.

Phthisic: asthma.

Plott Hound: a strong, rugged bear-hound bred locally by the Plott family.

Roastin' Ears: corn on the cobb.

Run: a marshy place or small stream, as in Tight Run, near Ravensford.

Scald: a bare hillside, sometimes a Fire Scald when the hill has been denuded of growth by fire.

Swag: a depression on a ridge, as in Big Swag on Round Mountain Ridge.

*P*roverbial comparisons and similes, because they appeal to the imagination or desire for novelty, are likely to spring up at any time and may travel far and wide; and some of the same expressions can be found almost any place in the country. But still a collection of them may have much local color and reflect the local personality. Some that I gathered in the Great Smokies are:

As Clean as a Hound's Tooth.

As Cross as a Sore-Tailed Bear.

As Bad as the Devil and Tom Walker: (probably suggested by the legend recorded by Washington Irving and others).

As Dead as Four O'Clock: "He killed the bear dead as four o'clock." Also "deader'n four o'clock." Is it possible that this phrase is connected with the four o'clock plant, one of the nightshades, which is said to have been used, broken up in milk, as a fly poison? More probably it refers to the hours of the dead, when ghosts walk, especially between midnight and dawn. This simile reminds us of the common saying "the dead of night" and Shakespeare's lines in *The Rape of Lucrece:*

> "Now stole upon the time the dead of night.
> No comfortable star did lend his light.
> No noise but owls' and wolves' death-boding cries."

As Dirty as a Hawg.

As Drunk as a Coon.

As Happy as a Dead Pig in the Sunshine.

As Ill Tempered as a Hornet

As Mad as a Wet Hen.

As Mean as a Black Snake.

As Plain as a Shoe.

As Pretty as a Speckled Pup under a Little Red Wagon.

As Tough as a Pigging String (said to be a rawhide string often used in tying the legs of a pig together before carrying it).

As Tough as a Pine Knot.

To Take Off like a Scalded Dog

To Scrouge over Like You Had a Family:

In trying to find a man in the Walland Creek section, I asked a boy what he looked like. He replied, " Like a skeered hant (ghost), I reckon." Uncle Mitch Sutton of Gnat Camp, near Mt. Sterling, said, "Old man Andy just looked like a forked stick with some britches on it." Frank Lambert, of Tow String Creek, who is a sixteenth Cherokee Indian and has just enough Indian blood to be allowed to live on the Qualla Indian Reservation (adjoining the park), told on a phonograph disc of a hunt in which he and his hunting companions fell in the creek on a very cold morning. He said, "Our britches legs was froze so we could feel the ice. They rattled just like tin." In asking someone on a couch or porch swing to move over to make room for others, one could say, "Scrouge over like you had a family." Of a stubborn person one hears. "He had a head like Collins' ram." Not very complimentary but apt is the saying, "He looked as sneaky as a sheep-killing dog", and one recognizes a certain descriptive truth in "Her tongue was goin' like a bell clapper."

A hunter once told me, "That bobcat was squallin' just like somebody."

Other comparative expressions are:

"Like the farmer's old mule, he just don't give a damn."

"Ain't that one more sight!"

When I met Neil Phillips of Muddy Holler, near Newport, Tennessee, and asked him in an interview how old he was, he answered, "I'm older than good." Later, in referring to his little grand-daughter who was playing in the yard in front of the porch where we were talking, he said, "She ain't bigger'n a cricket much." Jake Welch, of Hazel Creek, in telling on a disc of the good times he had before the national park came in, exclaimed, "God, we had one more time in this world a-bear huntin'!" Of one indefatigable story teller, a Roaring Fork man said, "He can tell more tales than John (referring to the Biblical John) told on the Isle of Patmos."

Some typical superlative expressions often heard are:

The Best Tickled I Ever Was.

That Was the Worst Ever I Was Scared.

He Was the Crabbedest Old Feller Ever I Seed.

Of similar picturesque effect are certain popular **"could"** and **"would"** expressions which are a kind of "tall talk":

He would steal the hat off your head, and you a-lookin' at him.

He could fit a circle sawmill. (Also common is "that feller would fight a circle saw."

A more direct imagery is found in a number of metaphorical words and phrases:

Captain: one who excels.

Catty: Active. "He's a catty old feller."

Clean Someone's Plow. To lick or punish. "I'll clean your plow" is a common warning to malefactors and to unruly children.

Devil's Kitchen: one woman's term for her husband's stillhouse.

Gentleman: An animal one is shooting at, said humorously.

To Get the Deadwood on Someone: To learn something about someone which he doesn't want people to know. A man can be pretty nice if you "have the deadwood on him."

To Give Someone the Eye: To show someone romantic interest.

To Groundhog It: To live in the poorest circumstances.

Headache or Toothache Medicine: liquor (veiled meaning).

To Jump the Broom: To get married, referring to an old protection against witches. As reported in Harry M. Hyatt, Folklore From Adams County, Illinois (New York, 1935), p. 372: "Let a bride jump over a broom just before she goes into her new home and she will never be 'hoodooed' there." Mrs. Polly Grooms of Newport, Tennessee, said, "Lay a broom across the door, and no witches won't step over that, they say."

Popskull: Rotgut Whiskey. "Popskull" is the name for low grade moonshine, a term now being replaced by the expressions "gray cloud" and "silver cloud", with reference to the "galvanize" (zinc) corroded from the "still" by the acid of the mash.

A Rough Old Coon: A hardbitten, aggressive old man; a hard fighter. Mr. George Lemons, of the Gumstand, told of General Morgan during the Civil War. He said, "He was a rough old coon. He made it in his mind to never surrender. He could fit a circle sawmill."

Watchin' His Bees or **Waitin' for His Bees to Swarm:** Euphemisms for expecting a baby. "John, when are your bees going to swarm?"

Joseph S. Hall

MOUNTAIN TALES:
The Murderous Innkeepers; An Old Folk Tale

*O*ne summer evening, following a clear day, storm clouds gathered swiftly and silently around Mt. Leconte. When, with sudden vehemence, they discharged their watery burden, the accompanying din was greater than the crash of thunder.

The next day was bright and clear as the morning sun shone over the drenched wilderness. Since there was some talk around the CCC camp of trails having been washed out by the cloudburst, the superintendent decided it would be wise to have an inspection of the Appalachian Trail between Newfound Gap and Dry Sluice Gap. Two foremen of the National Park Service were selected to go, and I was invited to make the trip with them. This was an ideal opportunity not only to traverse a portion of the Appalachian Trail connecting Maine with Georgia, but also to accompany two mountain men whose families have assumed prominent roles in the taming of a wild country to the orderly purposes of man.

It was on that long tramp that I heard the strange tale here related, a story once accepted by not a few people as true. The narrator, Lewis Reagan, said it was so old that few now knew it. He heard it from his mother, although it was also told, he said, by Jim Floyd, the son of the leading character.

Many years ago, on the trail between Sevierville and Gatlinburg (there was no road then), some people named Black operated an inn and made a practice of robbing those who stayed for the night. Unaware of this, a certain Art Floyd stopped there one evening to take lodging. He was conducted to a room, and, as he was preparing to retire, noticed that the windows were barred. Thinking this somewhat strange, he went to the door and found it would not budge. He was pondering what to do when he smelled a nauseating odor, and after a search about the room, he discovered the body of a man underneath his bed. It appeared to have been lying there for several days and showed marks of a violent beating. At that moment voices in the hall were audible. The uneasy prisoner heard the words, "Let's get him good!"

Quickly he dragged the body out, put it in the bed, and covered it with the bed clothes. Then he so placed himself as to be concealed by the door when it was

The author on a field trip to Cove Creek recording mountain folk songs. Singers Zeb and Winfred Hannah are in the background.

opened. Several men entered and set to hacking the body to pieces. Meanwhile, cautiously and unnoticed, Floyd slipped out of the room and fled from the place. At the nearest settlement he informed the "Law" of what was going on. Officers were dispatched to investigate. They arrived in time to arrest the murderers. A search of the premises revealed the graves of numerous other victims.

Later I mentioned this story to Sam Maples, a ninety-four year old veteran of the Union Army, who lived at the Gumstand. The Gumstand, a place on the road between Gatlinburg and Sevierville, was once a "stand" near a gum tree from which hunters shot game crossing the Little Pigeon River. Well acquainted with the folklore of the region, both he and the women folk of his household rejected the tale, claiming that without doubt it was circulated by some unsympathetic lowlander who found satisfaction in starting scandalous fictions about the mountain people.

That the tale enjoyed some currency, however, was revealed during a conversation with Jack Johnson, a resident of Dry Valley, Blount County, Tennessee, who, it was said, "can tell a great line of stories." Its quality as fiction was also brought to light, for the near-victim of his account was not Art Floyd, but one Captain Fry, and the setting was elsewhere.

Captain Fry, he said, lived in Haywood County, North Carolina, just across the mountains. One day, astride an "old jack", he was driving stock to South Carolina, and he had occasion to stop at an inn. He was shown to a room in which he soon found himself locked. Noticing an odor, he found the stiff body of a man under the bed. Then he heard someone in the hall say, "Let's make it a sure lick this time!" Placing the body on the bed, he hid himself beneath the bed on the floor. Men entered, hacked the body, and one of them observed that it did not bleed. Captain Fry managed to escape, got astride his jack, and was trying to urge the animal forward when he discovered that its ankles were bound with silk thread. He dismounted, cut the threads and then hurried away to notify the law.

Joseph S. Hall

MOUNTAIN TALES:
"The Worst Thing to Happen in these Mountains"
The Fate of Jasper Mellinger

*T*he worst thing to happen in these mountains, I reckon, was the death of Jasper Mellinger." This was the opinion of Lewis Reagan, fireguard in the National Park Service at Gatlinburg, Tennessee.

Mellinger, Reagan told me, was accidentally caught in a bear trap set by John Beasly. In violation of the law, this trap had been placed in the middle of a trail without warning signs. It broke Mellinger's leg and held him prisoner for about five days before Beasly returned with his son to investigate his catch. Seeing that Mellinger was almost at the point of death from pain and exposure, and fearing the consequences of what he had done, Beasly ordered his son to kill the unfortunate man with a small log lying nearby. The boy, at first revolted by the idea, finally complied with his father's request. The two of them placed Mellinger's body on a river bank and covered it with broken hemlocks. A few years later young Beasly fell mortally ill and on his deathbed confessed his crime.

Jim Cate, who lived on Little River above Elkmont, a point near which the death of Mellinger occurred, felt that Beasly was in no way responsible. Jim had talked to the detective who brought out Mellinger's bones, which were not discovered until three years after his death. Cate regarded young Beasly's confession as just a story. There was no evidence, he explained further, that Mellinger had ever been caught in a bear trap, whereas it was highly possible that he had broken his leg by stumbling, and died from exposure. Cate argued that the wound was too high on his leg to have been inflicted by a bear trap. He also pointed out that certain personal effects were found near the bones, including some money, a watch, and a rifle, and that John Beasly was too mean a man to leave these behind. A coroner's inquest was held at the scene of the death, but no true bill was issued by the grand jury. Apparently no circuit court was conducted.

Some time after hearing these accounts I struck up a conversation on the subject with a group of men who were lounging in one of the Lawson general stores in Wears Valley. I was told by a man who bore the name of Beasly, and who was related, presumably, to John Beasly, that the current story was false. He declared that it had been spread maliciously by enemies of the alleged murderer.

Reports of the inquest may no doubt be found in the local papers; but with the passing of time, such events are embellished with fancy in the popular mind, and become folklore.

Mellinger Death Ridge, a spur of Cold Spring Knob, on top of Smoky near Miry Ridge, by its name bears silent witness to the tragic event.

Joseph S. Hall

MOUNTAIN TALES:
Dead Man's Curve

*O*ne of the stories told in the vicinity of Mount Sterling is, through its quality of horror, likely to become traditional. It tells of the dynamite explosion on Big Creek in Walnut Bottoms when the road was being constructed above the old Crestmont logging camp. This road is now used by the National Park Service for fire control. That respected old mountaineer, Jake Sutton, formerly a fire guard, pointed out the spot as we drove over it. There is a huge rock cliff from which a passage has been blasted. This, he said, was Dead Man's Curve. This brief but pathetic tale explains the name (although one informant believed that the name already existed at the time, referring to a curve below this point where a man had been killed in a train wreck).

There were six men at work on the blasting. They were laughing and joking in a pause from work as they passed a bottle of' liquor from one to another. A hole had been drilled into the rock, and the dynamite was ready. Someone thrust into the opening a stick of powder, but it became "choked" (lodged) before reaching the bottom. When another worker tried forcing it with a crowbar, it exploded. Four of the men were blown to pieces.

Mrs. Neil Phillips, formerly of Barnes Valley and later of Muddy Hollow, near Newport, Tennessee, told me how her sons returned from work on the road that evening of the disaster. "They jes' come in, dropped down in chairs, n' never said a word. I studied what was the matter." Mrs. Hardy Sutton of Chestnut Branch, Big Creek, said: "They was four got killed. I reckon Hardy {her husband} holped (sic) pick up the pieces of their bodies."

Joseph S. Hall

MOUNTAIN TALES:
The Colorful Speech of Hunters

*S*tories and incidents told by hunters are usually striking because of their rugged, imaginative turns of phrases.

"Let me just blaze that gentleman (animal) by the right of the ear," said Ashley Moore of Walkers Valley, raising his long rifle (fashioned with primitive tools by a local artisan, but, like most such homemade firearms, accurate and powerful). He pretended to take aim as in the good old days, and then went on to tell of an incident at a hunting campfire: "A pan'ter (panther) was attracted by frying venison. In a thought or two it came out and screamed. Wouldn't come up wit in a shine of the fire." By "shine of the fire" is meant the reflection of light in the animal's eyes, making him a target at night. The eyes of many animals reflect light.

A "bear fight" is a fight between the dogs and a bear, or with the dogs baying and badgering it while the hunter waits for a chance to kill it without a dog. In a "bear race" the dogs try to catch up with the bear and corner it against a tree or a cliff. As the mountaineer describes it, they try to "hem the bear."

Joseph S. Hall
SOME ACCOUNTS OF MOUNTAIN WOMEN
"I've Spun Many a Thread" *Aunt Zilphie Sutton, Grannywoman*

Chestnut Branch lies within the National Park near its northeastern corner. It has its source on the southeastern side of Mt. Cammerer and contributes its waters to Big Creek, which, in turn, carries them not more than a few miles to the Pigeon River. Before the Park era about nine families lived on the branch, according to Mrs. Zilphie Sutton. As for nearby Walnut Bottoms, she said, "It was thick of houses, thick of people up thar then." On my visit to the area, only two families then remained. Mrs. Sutton, aged seventy, recalled that White Rock (now called Mt. Cammerer after a Secretary of the Interior) was once known as "Old Mother," a name also applied to Chestnut Branch. When she was a girl, her family would eat wheat bread on Sundays, but corn bread and potatoes during the week. "I seen a many, a many hard day with my brother. I've grubbed, split rails, and built fence."

"The 'No-Fence' law was the thing that ruint this country," Mrs. Sutton declared. She explained that, even though the land was owned by a lumber company, hogs were once allowed to roam at will over the mountains. The free-ranging of livestock, however, was brought to an end by the "No-Fence Law", the effect of which, contrary to the implication of the name, required the construction of fences by each landowner so that his stock might be confined to his own property.

Asked if the local women made the cloth needed for the clothing of their families when she was a girl, she replied, "I've spun many a thread and wove many a cloth." "Linsey", she said, was used for underwear. To dye the cloth "we biled warnut **(walnut)** bark and put copperas in it." After showing me how the carding and batting of cotton is done, she boasted, "I can bat enough cotton in a day to quilt a quilt."

She talked spiritedly of her home remedies. Up to this point in my interview it had been difficult to find topics upon which she cared to speak freely, but here she began in earnest, describing first the medical uses to which a number of well-known mountain herbs were put. "Catnip is the best thing in the world fer a risin'. Make ye a poultice of it. An' the tea's good to cool ye down. Fever weed breaks the fever on a body. Bone set's good to break the fever and a bad cold. Birth-root's good blood medicine. Indian physic tea is good to clean your stomach off. Hit's good blood medicine, too." Asked if she had taken much of it, she replied, "Lord, I've drunk a sight of it. Whenever we'd get puny, mother would go to the woods, gather some yerbs **(herbs),** and make us some tea."

For the croup and the phthisic she advised, "Take a sourwood switch, make a mark on it even with the top of the child'd head, lay it over the door, and let it stay there."

Furthermore, Mrs. Sutton told of her experiences as a "granny woman" or midwife: "I handled over two hundred babies," she declared. "I commenced when I was young. I was long-headed; wasn't afraid of nothin'. An' I never lost a woman in the whole boundary of 'em. I've catched them (babies) here, in Sunburst and in Kentucky." Asked where in Kentucky she had been a granny woman, she said, "Middlesboro, on yonder side of Cumberland Gap, where Kentucky and Buncombe County all jines together."

Actually, of course, Kentucky and North Carolina do not touch at all. Mrs. Sutton's conception of geography was somewhat hazy. Sunburst is a small town in Haywood County, North Carolina.

Joseph S. Hall

SOME ACCOUNTS OF MOUNTAIN WOMEN
Mrs. Debbie Mathis of Mingus Creek

*O*ver on the North Carolina side of the park, Mrs. Mathis was churning milk in a piggin, when I arrived following a two mile walk up Mingus Creek. A piggin is a small bucket made of wooden staves, one or two of the staves serving as handles. She was a rugged type of mountain woman and not any too ready to talk with strangers. I did succeed, however, in getting some information from her.

Eighty years of age at the time of my visit, she "was borned at Ravensford" and her parents were born on "Luftee" (the Oconaluftee River). Among the first settlers of Mingus Creek were Sam Finney and Hosey Rough, she said.

Encouraged to talk a little about old times in this district, she began: "In the old days the chimleys of houses was made of wood and daubed with mud. When we needed thread to sew and weave with, we'd have to send to Knoxville and trade corn and chestnuts fer it. We also raised flax and, after separatin' the flax from the tow, made thread."

She described the four grades of flour. The poorest was the "brans", which were fed to cows and hogs. Next came "shorts", which were used "to make the best pancakes." The "seconds" and the "good flour" were used to make bread.

As to Civil War times she mentioned the practice of keeping "home guards" to protect the lives and property of the local people. "Did you see any armies go through here?" I asked. "No," she replied, "we young-uns would shy (avoid) 'em." The Yankees once paid their house an unwelcome visit. "They just went in and sarched (sic) all over the house. Joel Connor and his wife buried their meat in the riverbank so the Yankees couldn't find it." I asked her how many were in the raiding party. "They was a pretty smart gang of 'em," she replied.

Home medicine was practiced in her family when she was a girl, but if the nature of the illness warranted, Dr. Mingus was called in. "Dr. Mingus was a rale (sic) good doctor," she asserted.

It is notable that Mrs. Mathis expressed sentiments unfavorable to the Union. Similar feeling was expressed by others, for example, "Grandmother" Enloe of Tight Run, Ravensford, North Carolina. The sympathies of the Smoky Mountain people were divided, the Tennesseans in general being pro-Union and the North Carolinians pro-Confederacy.

*E*xpressions of weather and time are always favorites with us, and so they have been in the Great Smokies. Newt Ownby of Elkmont, telling how a man got lost one time, explained, "The fog shut down on the mountain and ye couldn't see to travel." Zeb Crisp, of Hazel Creek, telling how he got caught in a storm while herding cattle on top of Smoky, said, "Just about dusky dark it was snowing like water pourin' out of a bucket."

Mrs. Bill Brown, of Ravensfork, suggested the winter beauty of a mountain forest: "Hit's the pertiest sight in the world when the snow covers the trees and you can see their shapes."

Old Dave Sparks of Cades Cove explained that the snowfall in the cove was light whereas it was heavy in the mountains roundabout: "Snow is shoe-mouth deep in the cove when's it's knee-deep in the mountains."

During a heavy rain one day in early summer, Sherman Meyers of Cades Cove said, "You can hear the corn grow." Weather often means bad weather, a rain or a snow storm. One may hear "We're goin' to have some weather," or "There's no need of you goin' out, it's so weathery." One way of explaining the phenomenon of snow is as follows: "The devil's whippin' his wife and all her feathers are comin' out," which has some interesting connections in folklore.

One summer day in Cades Cove, Sherman Myers and his wife took me to the site of the old family home. The building had been removed by the National Park Service, and the ground was overgrown with bushes and trees. But the old spring and some strawberry vines were still there. "I reckon that spring's worth a thousand dollars!" explained Mrs. Myers, with a feeling for her old home which only a displaced mountaineer may know. We enjoyed ourselves under the shade of trees and picked strawberries. There was a rumble of thunder on Gregory Bald overhead. "I reckon we'd orta be goin'," Mrs. Myers said. "Hit's lookin' a little rainy and the clouds are a-bilin' on them mountains."

And while the clouds are 'a-bilin'" on the Smokies, I reckon I'd "orta" be goin' too.

HARVEY BROOME

"I Have Never Wanted to Leave the Top of a Mountain"

Harvey Broome was a native son of the Smokies. Unlike Horace Kephart and Joseph Hall, Broome was born near the Great Smoky Mountains and started his love affair with them as a youngster growing up in Knoxville, Tennessee in the early part of this century. Born July 15, 1902, he could look out from the upstairs window of his home as a young boy and see the pale blue line of the Smoky Mountains forty miles distant.

Those mysterious first views of the mountains produced an unconscious yearning in him, something which was not intellectual or definable at his young age. It was more of an instinctive impulse, the kind of subconscious stirring that a person might experience when first looking up into the Milky Way Galaxy on a cloudless night and behold the immensity of the universe. Something in Broome's subconscious mind noted the existence of another fascinating world in the Appalachians. "I don't recall when I became aware that there were mountains to the south of Knoxville," he declared later in life. "But I could not have been very old." Only later, after he had been introduced to the backcountry by his father, did his yearning become identifiable as a love for the Smokies' wilderness.

Like Kephart and Hall, Broome also observed the mountain people in his wilderness travels. His earliest forays into the Smokies were in the late teens and early twenties of this century, so he encountered the hill people before the displacements caused by the establishment of the national park. His hikes around the Smokies took him "far past the last rough homestead where visitors were so rare that it was the prudent custom to pause outside the fence and call before approaching for fear of being shot." The American frontier obviously was still alive and well in these deep pockets of mountain wildness.

He also experienced the abuse of the mountain resources caused by unlimited timber cutting. The vivid memories of the destruction of the Smokies' forests which he saw as a lad provided the impetus for a lifelong conservation ethic, an orientation which eventually led Broome to a law degree and a career as a nationally recognized conservationist. His early Smoky Mountain days were always a foundation for his later professional challenges in conservation.

Broome entered Harvard Law School in 1926 (he unpretentiously declared later that he spent three years in "a law school in the east"), after graduating from the University of

Tennessee in 1923. He served as a law clerk for U.S. Circuit Judge Xen Hicks in 1930, and entered private practice in 1949. In 1958 he left private law practice and became a law clerk for U.S. District Judge Robert Taylor in Knoxville. This enabled him to devote more of his time to his real passion in life, the presidency of The Wilderness Society, a national conservation organization which he helped found.

His activity with the Society would be his real life's work, the focus for much of his energy and passion. He became engrossed in national conservation issues as president of The Wilderness Society, going beyond the Appalachian issues of his youth to questions of preservation in such faraway places as Jackson Hole, Wyoming and the Grand Canyon. He and other conservationists such as Bob Marshall, Howard Zahniser, Sigurd Olson, and Olaus Murie began to promote a grand concept of wilderness designation for public land, a concept which was a radical idea in the late 1940s and 1950s. It would take until 1964 for their dream of a national system of federally protected wilderness to become a reality. Broome, et al, must surely have despaired many times on the long, hard struggle to secure federal wilderness protection for appropriate land. What we take for granted today after the passage of the 1964 Wilderness Act was a laborious, frustrating struggle for these men as *they tried to sell the idea to the public and Congress.*

He and his wife Anna P. Broome purchased a cabin in Emerts Cove at the edge of the Smokies, a place which became their hermitage from the world of the city. Most weekends would find them either at the cabin or on the trails. The collective "we" in his writings always referred to his beloved wife.

From 1941 to his death in 1968 Harvey Broome kept what he called a "mountain journal" of his Smoky Mountain travels. He wrote a regular column for The Living Wilderness, *a publication of The Wilderness Society. He also wrote contributing chapters to several regional histories of east Tennessee, while having credits in* National Parks *magazine,* Nature *magazine and other periodicals. After his death, three collections of his writing were posthumously published, all now out of print:* Faces Of The Wilderness; Harvey Broome — Earth Man; *and* Out Under The Sky Of The Great Smokies, *the latter arguably the most philosophical reflection on the Smokies ever written.* Out Under The Sky Of The Great Smokies *has had the greatest impact on the interpretation of the Smokies wilderness, in the judgment of this editor. In it, Broome, the Harvard educated sophisticate who easily could have mixed with the rich and powerful of society, comes home*

to his east Tennessee roots and tells of the sweat, the pungent smells, the rain and snow, and the beauty of nature in the Smokies backcountry. As Benton MacKaye said of Broome's writings, "He will live in his works, gathering momentum as the need unfolds."

Come share Broome's love of the Smokies in the following passages from Out Under The Sky Of The Great Smokies.

HARVEY BROOME

Formative Years
(From *Out Under The Sky Of The Great Smokies*)

$\mathscr{F}$rom my birthplace on a hill in east Knoxville the Great Smoky Mountains were a pale blue band on the southern horizon. It is significant that my birthplace was also my own home. The town of Knoxville had only one hospital, seldom used for such natural events as births.

The majority of the streets were rutted surfaces of bare earth over which a layer of stone had been scattered. There were then few automobiles. People walked to their work, to school, to church, or rode the few electric trolleys. There were some private stables among the well-to-do. Bicycles were common, threading the treacheries of gravel and ruts. Sidewalks and a few downtown streets were of brick.

Most people read by the light of coal oil lamps or gas. Some streets were lit by gas — a few by the novel electric arcs. The daily newspapers and a few magazines kept the people aware of an outside world. The people read the Bible and the newspapers; went to church; went to bed early and arose early for the long ten-to twelve hour work days.

People took an interest in the churches and the new minister, in their children, in politics and elections, in shootings and murder trials, in fires which were frequent and destructive, and in deaths and weddings. There were modest excursions on the river, and boating was popular on the tiny lakes of the town park.

In this pleasant, peaceful, isolated, and self-contained world I don't recall when I first became aware that there were mountains to the south. But I could not have been very old.

As I have implied, the church was the center of much of the social life. The more sophisticated town churches sometimes chartered a train for their summer picnics. Cinders and black smoke poured in the open doors and windows of the swaying coaches, and the screech of the steam whistle raised the hair on our heads and allowed the cinders to settle closer to our scalps.

I loved the train rides. I loved the expectancy and the first lurch of the coach. One time we went beyond Maryville and rolled and jolted to the way-station of Walland, Tennessee. There our locomotive was detached, rolled onto a turntable, and was rotated by two straining trainmen. A curious engine with a battery of vertical pis-

March 17, 1935 — Harvey Broome on Ledge of the "Fort Harvey" Cliffs. Chimneytops in Background.

tons on the side was coupled on and we were jerked and towed for miles along a small river to Townsend.

This was a sawmill town. Everywhere were bark and lumber piles, and the sour tang of fresh sawed boards. I didn't question where the logs came from.

Beyond Townsend we entered a wooded gorge and were snaked up the stream. The wheels screamed on the curves. Such thrills! We looked down on raw boulders in water, foaming and clear. The cars crossed the stream on a bridge and everybody moved, as one, to the windows on the opposite side to continue a love affair with the river. It was alive and moving and beautiful.

Something was said about Elkmont {Ed. Note: Elkmont today is a national park campground and ranger station}. I know now that it was a logging camp, where there were some rough houses, a small railroad shop, and a commissary whose steps and floors were chewed and pitted by the needle calks in the Cutter boots of the lumberjacks. But we rolled on through Elkmont and were pulled a short distance beyond. We hardly had time for lunch and a furtive retreat to a screen of bushes to change our clothes for a quick, sharp dip into the clear biting waters. I didn't ask where the water came from.

I do not recall any particular impression made upon me by the rugged surroundings. I do recall that I was reluctant to leave when the long blast of the locomotive whistle signalled the end of the day.

As the train swept out through a deep water gap into the valley, the glorious facade of the mountains was broadside to the train. I leaned on the windowsill of the coach and watched that soft blue wall until it vanished in the twilight.

I had become aware that there were mountains. And after two or three such picnics at Elkmont, I became aware also that the pale blue band which could be seen from the upstairs front window of my birthplace was mountains.

Such was the first phase in the linkage of my life with mountains and the wilds. The second phase also had an early origin. Illness had touched the first decade and a half of my life. My body was frail, or so everyone thought; and I was shielded from contact sports. Though I performed my share of the chores — splitting kindling, carrying coal, cutting grass — I was undersized and weakly and a concern to my family.

In 1917, when I was fifteen, an uncle thought a camping trip in the mountains might boost my health. He approached my parents. Father agreed with alacrity; mother, who was always a cautious person, finally yielded to my enthusiasm for the trip.

The great day of departure started with a train ride to the Elkmont of earlier years. We were met by three grizzled mountaineers, whose clothes carried the odor of sweat and of the earth. The scent was not unpleasant but I was aware of it whenever I came near them, and the very experience was a part of this great new adventure.

Our mountain friends had three horses tied in the shade nearby. After an interminable period of weighing and balancing the bundles of duffle to the pack frames, we got under way. Our destination — twelve miles away and 3500 feet higher—was Silers Bald, near the heart of the Smokies.

Only the camping equipment was to be carried by the horses. The three mountain men, my three uncles, and a cousin and I were to walk. I was uneasy about the hike. I had no inkling of what was involved in walking twelve miles.

It was a hot August afternoon. Ridges towered to unbelievable heights. After climbing a few miles we digressed from the Jakes Gap trail to take the more direct, slippery and inhumanly steep Dripping Springs route to the summit of Miry Ridge.

Each of us was carrying an item or two which could not be packed handily on the horses. I had the rifle. Burdened with it and my own inexperience, my struggles in brief slippery spurts up the Dripping Springs mountain added nothing to my self-assurance. My legs were weak; my lungs were shallow. Every lunge upward seemed to bring me close to exhaustion. But the ascent finally dwindled away. The slope leveled off and we moved out on top of Miry Ridge.

That night we slept in a rude enclosure constructed around the "claim cabin" of a lumber company. We lay on the ground with only the folded canvas of a tent underneath us. A round moon arched across the sky. Stimulated by the openness above and by the hard earth beneath, as well as by the day's excitement, I slept little on this my first night, ever, out under the sky.

The next morning we started early. A mist hung close and in its dimness we and the horses wallowed the length of Miry Ridge. Pans clanged as packs collided with trees, and my cherished knapsack was torn on a snag. The morning was cool. The mist mingled with the forest in a muted world of rhododendrons and hemlocks, of birch and maples. By mid-morning it had vanished, and we emerged into sunshine at a rocky look-off near the junction of Miry Ridge and the Great Smoky divide.

The magnitude of the view was lost upon me. Every sight, except the punishing climb up Dripping Springs mountain, had been strange and exciting. The whole trip had been akin to a first breathless glimpse of the Grand Canyon. I had been plunged into wildness. When Uncle Charlie pointed out the one thing in that vastness of which I had previously heard — Silers Bald — I centered my attention on it.

About noon we pitched our wall tent on a little flat. Slender beech trees, cut from the forest, furnished poles for the tent and frames for our canvas cots. Sam Cook, our guide, found a small overhanging cliff and laid his bedding under it. Sam split bark from a buckeye, and flattening it out, made a table. A pole squared on one side and braced between two trees provided a seat. We assembled rocks for a fireplace. Our water was obtained from a scooped-out place down the side of the mountain. It was a long walk down, and it was a longer carry back with 40 to 50 pounds of water sloshing in lard cans between us.

A single layer of canvas discouraged the elements. We cut, chopped, and split trees for firewood. Candles provided light. The day's activities began with dawn and ended with the dark. There was no outhouse. One quickly found the pattern for more primitive ways. We experienced 48 continuous hours of rain and fog, and lived with mud and dampness. The rain falling on our tin plates splashed food into our faces. Smoke saturated our clothes as we rotated before the fire on a corduroy of logs laid to raise us above the mud.

On the east horizon four miles away was the rounded bulk of Clingmans Dome — what seemed to me a very high mountain. It was covered with an evergreen forest — denser, darker, and more mysterious than our grove of beeches. One fine day we followed the divide from Silers to Clingman. At one spot we looked far down into Tennessee and saw logging trains which resembled toys. At another spot we could both see and hear lumberjacks working in North Carolina.

At the summit of Clingmans we entered a dim, thickset stand of evergreens smaller than telephone poles. I did not inquire why the growth was different from the majestic deciduous forest, brilliant with wild flowers, through which we had ascended. But the memory of that dark and closely growing timber has remained with me all my life. Later I was to learn that it constituted a few acres of second growth and that there are differences between a primeval and a regenerating forest.

After two weeks we returned home. I had survived in the outdoors despite rain and bad weather. From Sam Cook I had discovered that one did not need a tent for a snug shelter but could use a cliff. I was sturdier and had gained a few pounds in weight. Under the sharp surveillance of three grown men I had been permitted to use an ax. But I could not have built a fire in the rain or have found my way without a guide. I had not learned what it meant to climb with a pack on my back.

On Silers we had been surrounded by a vast expanse of mountains, blue and inviting when the sky was clear. On the east rim was Clingmans Dome. Far to the west was Thunderhead. And on the north rim were the bold outlines of another great peak, Mt. LeConte. The huge triangle defined by those summits was a complete unknown world to me. My eyes were on Mt. LeConte, which had come to hold for me an irresistible appeal.

Three years were to pass before I was to climb it. The first World War intervened, curtailing much civilian activity but bringing one boon. Teenagers became a useful commodity upon the labor market and twice I worked for a short period at an apple orchard a few miles from the base of Mt. LeConte. This spot lay in tough foothill country, and a whole day by truck, wagon, and foot was consumed in covering the forty miles between Knoxville and the orchard.

The mountains were close and twice we took quick trips around the end and back of LeConte to a stream of surpassing beauty. We hiked far past the last rough homestead where visitors were so rare that it was the prudent custom to pause outside the fence and call before approaching for fear of being shot.

Here we purchased eggs and obtained permission to use a cabin belonging to a lumber company. Beyond the cabin we entered upon an old trail which had served as access to saltpeter deposits in the Civil War. Since that date it had had limited use for passage between North Carolina and Tennessee. Overgrown and narrow, the trail crossed and recrossed a stream of absolute clarity.

The crossings I approached with real fear. We were backpacking and I reached the stream with rubbery legs and scorched lungs. There were no footlogs, and we waded or leaped from boulder to boulder. If a person slipped, or his knapsack pulled him off balance, he would bang a shin or fall into the water. On the Silers Bald trip my introduction to mountains had been along their ridge tops, but now I received my baptism in their streams.

Our destination was a tiny log cabin which had been erected in a rough clearing above the stream. The gaps between its logs were closed by clean, hand-split shingles which had been nailed horizontally on the inside. The work was crude, and the air circulation remained excellent. The cabin had a puncheon floor and a roof of split shingles.

A small iron stove with a flat cooking surface was propped on billets in one corner of the cabin. Pole bedsteads with corn husk mattresses occupied two corners, and a pile of firewood, mostly waste from the cabin construction, was stacked handy to the stove. This was our shelter.

We fished the stream for brook trout. One of my companions was an expert who caught all that we could eat. Our fire of hemlock and spruce chunks popped and crackled as it flickered through the cracks in the stove. The smoke of these woods also has an extreme pungency, and the night breezes swirled it like incense both outside and inside the cabin with separate but equal abandon. At nightfall the vastness

August 1922 — On the top of Mt. LeConte (Harvey Broome, right; Simon Marcovitch, left)

and darkness of the uncut forest settled about us, and our whole world centered around the liveliness in that rickety stove. The high beech woods and meadows of Silers Bald had never been like the overwhelming, inky-black forested wilderness at the bottom of that narrow, chill, north-facing valley.

After the camping trip I worked again at the orchard. In good weather the summit of LeConte was visible eight tantalizing miles distant and 5000 intriguing feet higher. On the weekend before I was to return to Knoxville to the university, I planned to make the climb with some mountain friends. Quite unexpectedly my father appeared on the day before, and quite characteristically joined the party. He knew that his way of life had not conditioned him for such a trip. But he lived his life with a certain elan, often counting the cost of an adventure afterward rather than before. I have always been grateful that he turned up to share this climb with me.

There was a trail less than half the way. When it played out we took the first hollow to the right. And when it became impassable from vertical cliffs made slippery by moss and water, we bore to the left to the ridge on that side of the gulch.

We were now on the side of Mt. LeConte itself and again encountered cliffs and maddening thickets of laurel and rhododendron. We scrambled and we slipped; we clawed and we pulled. This lofty mountain seemed to have no summit, and I was becoming weak from hunger and fatigue. When it seemed I could go no further I dragged myself over a low ledge and found we had reached the top.

The view from the immediate summit was disappointing because of a screen of balsams. But after lunch we fought our way to a look-off point, and a truly magnificent and tremendous view burst upon us. We were on one of the points of the great triangle of which Silers was the center. But the superior elevation and location of LeConte produced stupendous views not only of mountains but of the fields and hamlets in the Great Valley {Ed. Note: The Great Valley of the Tennessee River}. Though the day was brilliant, to the north over Knoxville was a long sooty band touching the horizon. I had not then heard of smoke pollution.

The middle peak, or Cliff Tops, to which we proceeded after lunch, was covered with dense stands of windswept balsams, a low growing rhododendron, and masses of a gorgeous, hedge-like shrub with tiny glistening leaves suggesting a boxwood — Huger's sand myrtle. The leaves of this resplendent plant had a waxy content and were highly flammable. This fact was discovered by the youngest member of the party, who set fire to an isolated clump. He was scolded by his father who quickly stamped out the blaze.

But when we left the cliffs for the descent this youngster lingered. Later when we looked up from the open summit of the Rocky Spur far below, we saw a column of white smoke hovering over Cliff Tip. The sand myrtle was afire and I felt a youthful outrage. For the first time in my life I had wanted to protect a bit of nature from destruction.

We followed no trail down the mountain, as we had followed one but little on the ascent. This trip had been an introduction to bushwhacking by my mountain friends who were masters of the art. My fears of the unknown and of getting off a trail had been blunted. The experience led to an awareness that every foot of the mountains was open to me, and that trails, though a convenience, were not a necessity. And on the same trip a lifelong concern for the vegetative cover of this land was kindled by that senseless blaze in the sand myrtle on Cliff Tops on top of Mt. LeConte.

The next years had their frustrations. I was busy at the university and plagued by lack of time and money. Once or twice I managed a prodigious excursion, prompted equally by my love of the mountains and by my desire to measure myself against them.

At Easter we skipped classes and took a trip to Thunderhead — the massive grassy bald which had formed the western tip of the great triangle revealed from Silers (Bald). This was a 40 mile jaunt crowded into three days. We were elated by seeing acres of bird's-foot violets in the foothills and by the sight of a yellow lady's slipper — my first orchid. Soft from unwonted exercise, we had crammed six months of yearning into one relentless excursion.

Another summer I worked at the very base of Mt. LeConte. My employer was versed in botany. From him I learned the identity of many trees in this land of many trees. On the weekends his home became an overnight stop for visitors from the "outside" who coveted a look at these great, verdant, little known mountains. On one weekend two research professors, a botanist and an entomologist, were there. From them I learned the name of the fresh and beautiful pink turtlehead, a flower which grew near the summit of Mt. LeConte.

On another weekend a taxonomist of some note came from a mid-western college.

His excitement, as he discovered plant after plant which he had not even seen before, was contagious. In the party that day were several mountaineers. During a rest our visitor reached down and picked a leaf of the dog hobble which covered a whole slope. Musingly, half to himself, he spoke its scientific name, <u>Leucothie</u>.

One of the mountain men replied, "'Leucothy,' that's what we calls it." Who was the ancestor who had known and handed down the scientific name of this shrub, and why had he come to these mountains?

One autumn I departed East Tennessee for three years at an eastern law school. I came home each summer and worked in a law office, but managed a trip or two to the mountains.

On one of these we hiked from Thunderhead to Clingmans Dome, camping along the way. Sam Cook was again our guide. At Spence Field we found many domestic animals grazing on its expansive summit meadows, the practice of valley farmers being to summer their stock in the mountains.

At our campsites I learned from Sam how to start a fire, how to set up a crane from which to hang a bucket over the fire. At Buckeye Gap we heard a call in the night.

The eyes of young John Tittsworth widened with fear.

"What's that?"

Sam chuckled, "That's an owl; he's your friend."

The "whoo whoo" of this bird is one of the startling sounds of the great woods. Its call is yet heard in many areas of our country. Where there are woods enough for it, there is hope for wilderness.

The next day we all hiked to Elkmont via Miry Ridge. As we descended through the rain there was smoke in the air and we began to see blackened stumps and snags. The area had been logged, had burned, and was still smoldering. I could not perceive in this open, rocky, charcoal-black area, the lush and magnificent forest I had traversed in mist eight years earlier. Down in the hollow we ran into the logging operation itself in a land I had known under different conditions on my first trip into the high mountains. I had found the origin of the logs which fed the sawmill at Townsend. The following summer, at Charlies Bunion, I was again to see first-hand the consequences of careless logging.

Whereas Mt. LeConte had once been my great goal, I now wanted to try Mt.

Guyot, a peak second in height only to Clingmans Dome and located in a remote complex of mountains far to the east of LeConte. I had interested Wiley Oakley in going with me. He was a mountaineer who looked upon the mountains as a source of beauty and inspiration, rather than as a resource to be exploited.

We were to hike from Gatlinburg to LeConte and out the meanders of the ridge, now known as the "Boulevard," to the state line, and thence along the untrailed state line to Guyot.

The Boulevard ridge was trailless. We were slowed by frightful undergrowth and by the battering of a summer storm. By late afternoon we had barely reached the edge of the burn near Charlies Bunion, on which were now stands of blackberry briers eight feet high. We plunged into them hoping to reach Dry Sluice Gap by dark, but were held back by the briers and by partially burned trees which had fallen across our course. The briers had completely engulfed the windfalls so that we were unaware of them until we walked into protruding limbs. Progress was slowed to a quarter of a mile an hour.

Near the gap the briers thinned a bit. We attacked blackened logs with an ax and chopped out dry wood for our camp fire.

A second storm struck and we thatched the fire with bark. But there was no dry spot for sleeping. Finally we collected large stones and heated them in the fire. Some of these we placed at our feet and others on the slope as seats. I shall never forget Wiley's tentative test, and how quickly he sprang upright when he found the seat too hot. Over this spot we stretched a poncho and sat out the night.

Dawn eventually came. Our eyes were red from smoke and sleeplessness; our hands and faces were scratched and besmudged. We decided to return to Gatlinburg by the shortest route. This was down the trail from Dry Sluice Gap, and through the Porters Flat of the Greenbriar.

On the descent we followed a deep ravine just east of the Charlies Bunion peaks and ridges. Looking up at them, we were appalled. They had been incinerated down to the bare rock leaving only the blackened trunks of a once virgin forest. Since there had been no logging on the Tennessee side, the fire must have started in the loggings in North Carolina. It had swept across the divide into several hundred acres of virgin woods in Tennessee.

Two miles farther, the valley leveled out into the Porters Flat where grows one of the surpassing deciduous forests on earth. It was as unspeakably beautiful as the area of holocaust had been unutterably blighted.

In the decades following the first Silers trip I grew in assurance and strength. My love for mountains and wild country became a major motivation. My trips there numbered into the hundreds in every season — from the cold dormance of winter, through the perfections of spring and the heavy humidity of summer, to the sharp scintillating delights of fall. They involved short one-day excursions and week-long backpacks. Camp fires were built from wood so damp that moisture pockets, exploding in the wood, blew out the flames. Camps were established in storms so violent that they dumped four inches of rain in a night. I waded streams so cold that my feet became numb, pushed through snow up to my middle, and camped in the deep forest at temperatures of -15°F.

My knowledge grew not only of the terrain of the mountains but of their plant and animal life. Recognition of first- and second-growth forest developed, and likewise perception of the succession of plants involved in the long journey back from disturbance to climax forest. The differences between north-slope and south-slope vegetation became clear.

The movement for a National Park in the Great Smokies got under way during an absence of mine. But upon my return to Knoxville I supported Colonel David C. Chapman and other leaders of this complex and successful undertaking.

In 1930 I learned of the Appalachian Trail and participated in the location of remote stretches of the trail through the mazes of little known ridges in the Smokies.

I became acquainted with Benton MacKaye, father of the Appalachian Trail; with Stanley Cain, a great and articulate ecologist; with Robert Marshall, a professional forester and a towering figure in the field of wilderness preservation; and with Bernard Frank, a specialist in forest influences, from whose searching eyes little escaped.

On trips into the mountains with these and many others, there came a disturbing awareness of the rift between the untrammeled wilds and the rifled countryside where man had established his civilization. It was not enough to enjoy wild country; one felt compelled to try to conserve and defend the land against further spoliation.

With MacKaye, Marshall, Frank, and four other conservationists, I was associated in the founding of The Wilderness Society.

Some persons hunt for the origins of the wilderness movement in the consciences of big city dwellers, who, seeing about them the shambles of the natural world, seek to protect and restore it elsewhere. But my own beginnings in a provincial valley town, and my youth among a gentle and unassuming people, rebut such a sweeping assumption. The very first time I journeyed the few miles from my home village to the foothills of the Smokies, I found something beautiful, different, and intensely desirable. I had not been conditioned by the fevers of a metropolis. The great bent of my life had been fixed before I set foot beyond the boundaries of Tennessee.

April 30, 1941. I wish I could re-experience the awe I once had for that great ever-changing facade of Mt. LeConte. In 1920 I walked back and forth from George Ogle's to the Watson home with my eyes glued on its vast bulk which I had never climbed. Then came my first climb, when I nervously wondered whether I would have the strength to make the top. Later came a second climb, by way of Bear Pen Hollow, when I first experienced the sight of clouds drifting through the trees just above my head. Fearfully I wondered whether we would lose our way should they envelop us.

In the intervening years the great outlines and moods and framework of the mountains have become familiar. Those early unknowns have yielded to subtler ones which move and pass us by and vanish. I think of the sigh of the wind in the tops of the high spruces, one of the most haunting sounds I know. I try to seize upon the soft yellow-green wash of spring. It fades even while I observe it.

The mountain streams roar and swirl on through eternities, gathering incessantly in the chill clefts of the high ridges, renewing themselves unceasingly from the heavy falling rains. They go on and on, while we watch and while we don't watch.

I have thought that the word **America** must mean different things to the people who live under its aegis. I would that for each of them it might be symbolized by one — at least one — memory of some aspect of unspoiled nature. America — wide, far-reaching, insouciant — has been the amphitheatre for our civilization. I wish each of us could appreciate its vast beauty, and could see how far the elements of our civilization fall short of the sheer majesty of our America.

It is curious to think that if by some calamity our civilization should pass away, or be eclipsed or uprooted and cast out, America the land will continue on its slow, imponderable geologic heavings; that the plants eventually will reach out and seize and cover and heal the raw slopes we have so improvidently ripped open; that the bird life which somehow lives with us, and yet above and beyond us, will return in abundance and merriment; and that our great dams will crack, seep dry, and disintegrate before timeless forces of frost and rain and sun.

May 7. 1941. The spell of Sunday's hike up Buck Fork and over to Ramsay {Ed. Note: Ramsay Cascade} is beginning to wear off under the bludgeoning of city life. Incessant noise, auto horns, the whine of electric trolleys, pneumatic drills, and sirens have supplanted the peace of the wilds.

At the crest of the ridge on Sunday we emerged into a flat mossy spruce woods, which reminded me of High Top on Mt. LeConte in the old days. One wonders if this was the first time man had ever edged through this copse, for we had missed a turn and were a mile east of where we should have been. We were recompensed for

Harvey Broome, 1957.

our mistake by coming upon that silent stand of boreal forest.

I yearn now to move along the length of that ridge, through the great aisles in the rhododendron at Drinkwater Gap, to the fir thickets on Guyot itself. It must be one of the least frequented places in the Smokies — the land of the bear and of the winter wren and of the sad winds.

September 24, 1942. Last weekend, starting out from Knoxville under an overcast sky, we moved toward the mountains under increasingly heavy clouds. The mist hit us short of Emerts Cove, and the rest of the day we were either in rain or heavy mist.

How we cringed at first from the damp bushes and undergrowth — but by the time we reached the end of the trail along Porters Creek it made little difference whether we avoided them or not. We were by then well soaked. Progress up the Charlies Bunion Prong was rapid. A second flood had gouged out some of the accumulations of the '27 deluge and we moved easily over the open rock. I was wearing Bean boots and was concerned for my footing on the rocky slopes and cliffs of the Bunion higher up. I needn't have worried. The rock was clean-sharp, and only occasionally did

I find a film of lichen or moss. For the most part I climbed as securely as though my feet at each step were glued to the rock. Although we moved in rain and through dirty white fog and were met by a merciless wind on the ridge crest, I have never made the climb more easily. A few times we dislodged scree, and once or twice a fallen tree moved as we passed over it, but otherwise my climbing was serene.

Some of the boys climbed in shorts, and as they dallied to let others catch up they shook with cold. We couldn't see 75 feet ahead of us. The slopes dropped off hideously steep each way from the narrow crest, to be lost in a foggy void. As we progressed upward, the Bunion took shape out of the fog in a dark precipitous blot.

Seven of us reached the top and plowed down through the underbrush to the trail. There the wind tore greedily at our bodies and even those of us who were warmly clad began to chill. Three of the party were lagging unaccountably down that fog-wrapped ridge and I pushed back through the bushes to investigate. By this time it was raining hard and my clothes had become completely saturated. The water gleamed where my trousers stretched over my knees and thighs. I reached the unsheltered crest and met a wind so blasting that when I shouted it seemed to blow my voice back down my throat. As I strained for a possible answering shout, the wind roared across my ears drowning out all other sound.

I climbed down the rocks a hundred feet or so, braced myself, and called again. No answer. I began to shake convulsively. I couldn't see. The wind shook me and I was chilling rapidly. I could hardly have been more alone, more buffeted, had I been on Everest.

Eventually we met up with the missing hikers at Newfound Gap and all of us returned to Knoxville together.

June 26, 1945. Saturday night I lay out on the sward of Gregory Bald. Three of us were 50 yards down on the North Carolina slope to escape a sharp and incessant breeze. A full moon followed an arc across the southern heavens. No dew collected on the grass. We lay on and between hummocks of grass. Near mountains were dark; far ones were lost in a blue-gray murk. Clumps of azalea, with color obscure, stood sentinel about us. All the world we could see lay below the rounding bald. Here was spaciousness, moon-blue beauty, and infinite space. No sound but the wind; no sight but the aloof and elusive and painfully beautiful natural world. And while George Hines and Guy slept, their inert and shapeless forms bulking monstrously in their sleeping bags, I sat up, deep in the night, and looked.

Here was the break needed between individual man and his civilization. One becomes humble, alone with the wind in a prodigious circle of mountains. Values and incentives clarify; the transiency of man becomes painfully manifest; and self-ishness and ignorance seem unworthy before this impersonal and inscrutable vastness. I had no feeling of wanting to retreat from it, but rather of broadening my own spirituality to encompass more of it. Only the richest and boldest of civilizations are worthy of the earth to which they cling so fitfully.

October 31, 1948. Last Sunday I relaxed upon some uneven ground at the Rich Mountain fire tower. The air was fitful and blustery. Clouds raced across the sky holding back the warming rays of the sun. Even wearing many clothes, I was not quite comfortable in the shadows. Lying on the ground, hat over my eyes, my body sharply sensitive, I listened to the incessant stirring of the wind in the dead leaves of the oaks. There was no surcease — a continuous ferment of sound which left me vaguely dissatisfied.

What did it mean? Why did the wind blow? Listening, I was not a part of it. The air would have surged and the leaves rustled, whether I was there or not. It was building up to no climax. A cool front was coming in, but that is just a description, not an explanation. There was something inscrutable, elusive, about this noisy activity in which I joyed, but which I could not interpret. Winds blow where they list, seemingly without end, dropping into a calm or bounding into violence like the moods of a giant and everlasting symphony.

February 14, 1956. Last Sunday I went to White Rock (now called Mt. Cammerer). Clouds lingered over some of the mountain tops, but others were resplendent in the sun. White Rock was clear. Valleys and draws along the north side of the Pinnacles Lead and Old Smoky were dim and haunting. The sun gleamed on the hoarfrost along the crests and threw impenetrable shadows into the hollows.

We started hiking immediately. The cold air burned our lungs and foreheads. The streams were dashing, and although they originated in second growth they were sparkling and transparent.

The country through which we were ascending had not been long abandoned. Old apple trees were still conspicuous in young forests of hemlock and pine, peawood, and red maple. But there was unexploited vastness upstream, and it showed in the brooks and runs.

We climbed rapidly over a cushion of needles and leaves. The old sled road which we first followed had no raw slopes and was almost completely shielded with leaves and vegetation. The trail, a simple man-way, had not been scraped or graded. Even where it was very steep, there was little erosion. There was a healing cleanliness to it.

Sooner than I thought possible, we passed through the first belt of pines and edged into a band of deciduous growth. Immediately we heard the wind roaring as it rushed through the bare limbs. It was violent, sustained, deep, and powerful. The sound made me want to shout madly.

On the exposed rocky summit, the very air sparkled. The wind had stilled. The mountains were blue and sharp-lined. Clouds hung on the southern and western horizons in broken horizontal layers like great dingy galleons with white decks and white foam where they break the water. This rocky crag dominated the landscape for many miles. One became heady with a sense of easy power as he had but to turn his head to look down upon miles and miles of the human world.

After lunch there was an unplanned gathering in a sunny pocket among the rocks. We got to reminiscing, drawing on decades of memories of experiences shared together. Laugh followed laugh like waves breaking on the shore. Sun and companionship were warm—the memories dear and choice. Can life at its finest offer more than this brilliant nexus of man and mountains? Will man ever be really happy until he restores to his daily environment the unstudied beauty and divine peace of the natural world? **I have never wanted to leave the top of a mountain ...**

ARTHUR McDADE

*O*ne afternoon in early October I was driving up Highway 441, the Newfound Gap Road, in the Great Smoky Mountains National Park. I rounded a curve and saw, for perhaps the 200th time, the sharp peaks of the Chimney Tops in the distance.

Now, I had climbed "the Chimneys" many times before, but the thought still crossed my mind, "Why not today?" It was a wonderfully clear fall day, and I knew the view would be fabulous. But I had places to be and miles to drive, and it was already 4 p.m. My rational mind said, "No, we need to keep on driving."

An hour later I puffed my last deep breath and sat down on the rocky knob of the upper Chimney. The climb had been two miles from the trailhead, but I had hiked fast. It had been over a year since I had last climbed here, and more than a decade since climbing cross-country with the Smoky Mountain Hiking Club one cold December day. Once again the incredible mountain scenery overwhelmed me. For over an hour I sat on the exposed peak with no one around and marvelled at the view. I was glad I had changed my plans.

The immense massif of Mt. LeConte dominated the landscape in front of me. I studied its ridges. I could see Clifftops and Myrtle Point at the top of the mountain. I could visualize the ridge where the Boulevard Trail from Newfound Gap comes to the apex of the peak. To the northwest, I gazed down the long green valley of the West Prong of the Little Pigeon River, a valley that was heavily logged by timber companies in the early part of this century. It was an incredible view.

Harvey Broome, the grand old man of the Smokies, described the Chimney Tops and the surrounding mountains in the book Out Under The Sky Of The Great Smokies:

> "Yesterday we hiked again to the Chimneys, to a spot which in one way or another has been a part of my life for over 40 years. I believe it was 1918 that I took my first trip up the West Prong of the Little Pigeon River and caught my first view of the Chimneys. No one had warned me of these precipitous and distinctive peaks. I was hiking along on a fishing trip, trying to keep up with the others, and glanced up. 'What are they?' I cried, astounded by their sharp points and vertical slopes. Someone said, 'The Chimney Tops.' I am sure that I resolved right then and there to climb them, although it was more than two years before I made the opportunity.

Arthur McDade and Father in front of Chimney Tops, Summer, 1953 — Great Smoky Mountains National Park

"I climbed the Chimneys first with Uncle Charlie Mooers and his son George in 1920. Since those first climbs, the Chimneys, the Road Prong, the dark silent pools, the gleaming foam of the little cascades — Alum Cave, LeConte, the whole general area — have become deeply involved in my life. These wonderful, beautiful mountains are as much a part of me as my bloodstream, or the hand which traces out these words."

Sitting on top of the Chimneys that October day, I finally realized that it was getting late, and I did have places to be that evening. I reluctantly turned and scrambled down the rock face to the ridge and started down the trail.

As I walked contentedly down the trail in the coolness of the early October evening, listening to the Road Prong sing its water song, I thought of Horace Kephart, Joseph Hall and Harvey Broome and their work in describing the Great Smoky Mountains. As I walked and thought, I found myself agreeing wholeheartedly with Harvey Broome. These "wonderful, beautiful mountains" are indeed "as much a part of me as my bloodstream."

Acknowledgements

Generous and substantial assistance came from the following people: Steve Kemp of the Great Smoky Mountains Natural History Association, who encouraged the project; Gene Cox, Chief of Interpretation in Great Smoky Mountains National Park, who reviewed the manuscript and offered erudite suggestions; Glen Cardwell, Park Ranger in the Smokies; Annette Evans, librarian in the park; William S. Broome, nephew of Harvey Broome, and his son, Dr. William Broome; Wayne Kramer, Attorney At Law, and Executor of the estates of Harvey and Anne Broome; Harvey Hall and Helen Hall, brother and sister of Joseph S. Hall; Dr. Michael Montgomery of the University of South Carolina; George Frizzell of Western Carolina University; Sally Polhemus of the East Tennessee Historical Society; the late Valary Marks, editor of *The Tennessee Conservationist*, for permission to excerpt parts of the Epilogue. David Morris ably worked on the layout and graphics for the book. Special thanks for advice and guidance to Charles Maynard, a master Appalachian storyteller, writer, and Executive Director of the Friends Of The Great Smoky Mountains.

Finally, thanks to the people of the Smoky Mountains who lived their unique lives and gave us the rich cultural heritage of those "Old Smoky Mountain Days."

Other Books Which Tell of the Old Days in the Smoky Mountains

IN THE SHADOW OF OLD SMOKY by C. Hodge Mathes
A delightful recounting of stories and tales by a wonderful writer who lived and worked in the mountains from the 1880s to 1950s. Prof. Hodge Mathes taught languages at Maryville College, East Tennessee State University and Milligan College. His stories bring to life the people of a by gone era.

IN THE SHADOW OF OLD SMOKY An audio tape of four of Mathes's best stories as told by master storyteller Charles Maynard.

IN THE SPIRIT OF ADVENTURE
   A 1914 Smoky Mountain Hiking Journal by D.R. Beeson
   A 1915 Mt. Mitchell Hiking Journal by D.R. Beeson
   A 1913 Roan and Grandfather Mountains Hiking Journal by D.R. Beeson
   A 1914 Table Rock Mountain Hiking Journal by D. R. Beeson

This collection of four books are the hiking journals and photographs of D. R. Beeson of Johnson City, Tennessee. Beeson and his hiking partner, C. Hodge Mathes, walked through the mountains long before trails, roads and parks. This collection preserves the witty and precise observations of one who truly loved the mountains.

Panther Press has many other titles pertaining to the Smokies and nature topics. For more information or a catalogue write:

Panther Press
P.O. Box 636
Seymour, Tennessee 37865
423-573-5792
Fax 423-573-5697